THE **MINI** ROUGH GUIDE TO
BOLOGNA

ROUGH GUIDES

YOUR TAILOR-MADE TRIP
STARTS HERE

Tailor-made trips and unique adventures crafted by local experts

Rough Guides has been inspiring travellers for more than 35 years. Leave it to our local experts to create your perfect itinerary and book it at local rates.

Don't follow the crowd – find your own path.

HOW ROUGHGUIDES.COM/TRIPS WORKS

STEP 1 Pick your dream destination, tell us what you want and submit an enquiry.

STEP 2 Fill in a short form to tell your local expert about your dream trip and preferences.

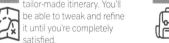

STEP 3 Our local expert will craft your tailor-made itinerary. You'll be able to tweak and refine it until you're completely satisfied.

STEP 4 Book online with ease, pack your bags and enjoy the trip! Our local expert will be on hand 24/7 while you're on the road.

PLAN AND BOOK YOUR TRIP AT
ROUGHGUIDES.COM/TRIPS

HOW TO DOWNLOAD YOUR FREE EBOOK

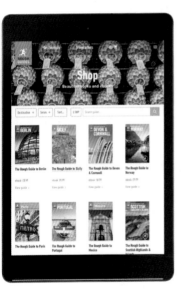

1. Visit **www.roughguides.com/free-ebook** or scan the **QR code** below

2. Enter the code **bologna907**

3. Follow the simple step-by-step instructions

For troubleshooting contact: mail@roughguides.com

10 THINGS NOT TO MISS

1. SANTO STEFANO
Enchanting complex of medieval churches, cloisters and crypts. See page 47.

2. LE DUE TORRI
The Two Towers are iconic symbols of the city. Climb to the top of tilting Torre degli Asinelli for splendid views of the city. See page 42.

3. MAMBO
A sleek contemporary arts centre filled with experimental works. See page 64.

4. THE PORTICI
Bologna's elegant porticoes span an incredible 38km (24 miles) through the city's historic centre. See page 37.

5. GASTRONOMY
Indulge in Bologna's culinary delights and find out why they call the city 'La Grassa' (The fat). See pages 91 and 100.

6. NEPTUNE'S FOUNTAIN
Giambologna's show-stopping bronze of Neptune is a favourite meeting place for the Bolognesi. See page 30.

7. SAN LUCA
Climb the world's longest portico to the hilltop sanctuary church of San Luca. See page 72.

8. PALAZZO DELL'ARCHIGINNASIO
Former seat of the city university, with a seventeenth-century anatomical theatre where human corpses were once dissected. See page 38.

9. BASILICA DI SAN PETRONIO
The monumental basilica ranks among the most imposing of Italy's Gothic churches. See page 34.

10. PINACOTECA NAZIONALE
The city's finest art collection featuring works by Bolognese and other Italian masters. See page 56.

A PERFECT DAY

9am

Breakfast. Kick off the day with coffee and a *brioche* at *Caffè Sette Chiese* on Piazza Santo Stefano. Secure a seat beneath the stone arches of the portico for fine views of Santo Stefano. After breakfast, wander through the delightful jumble of medieval churches, cloisters and courtyards.

10am

Strada Maggiore. From Via Santo Stefano, duck down the Corte Isolani, a quaint warren of galleries and cafés, to Strada Maggiore where porticoes and palatial homes line the street. Browse the antique shops before eyeing up the foreboding Gothic Church of Santa Maria della Vita.

11am

Historic core. Head for Piazza del Nettuno, watched over by Giambologna's immense bronze statue of Neptune, and beyond to Piazza Maggiore, where fading palazzi crouch beside the hulking Basilica di San Petronio; peek inside the monumental interior of the vaulted church.

Noon

Culinary delights. Lose yourself in the maze of narrow alleys off Piazza Maggiore to stumble across tantalizing delis, market stalls and a chic covered food hall. For lunch, grab a *piadina* crammed with Parma ham, *Mortadella* and local cheeses, or head to *Tamburini* at Via Caprarie 1, a gourmet deli-café that's been winning over foodies since 1932.

2pm

Ancient university. Meander down Via dell'Archiginnasio, where porticoes shelter elegant designer stores. Visit the

IN **BOLOGNA**

frescoed Palazzo dell'Archiginnasio, first seat of Europe's oldest university and where, in the Teatro Anatomico, some of the earliest dissections in Europe were performed.

3pm

Leaning towers. Head northeast to the Due Torri and gawp at the tipsy towers. Climb the calf-shredding 480 steps to the top of Torre degli Asinelli for fine views over the reddish sea of clay rooftops. Stroll around the nearby former Jewish Ghetto, now home to a cluster of artisan workshops.

4pm

University quarter. Amble along Via Zamboni for a flavour of the university. Pass noble palazzo converted to temples of scholarship, bohemian bars, cafés and arty bookshops.

6pm

Aperitivo time. Head to *Le Stanze*, the private chapel of the Palazzo Bentivoglio reimagined as a cocktail bar (Via del Borgo di San Pietro 1), where you can sip on colourful concoctions surrounded by sixteenth-century frescoes.

8pm

Dinner. Feast on traditional Bolognese pasta, made on the spot before you, at *Dal Biassanot*, Via Piella. Beside the *trattoria*, peer through the Finestrella di Via Piella (tiny window) over the canal and you might believe you were in Venice.

10pm

Jazz in the cellar. Round off the evening with the best live jazz in Bologna at *Cantina Bentivoglio*, Via Mascarella 4/B, in the antique cellars of the Palazzo Bentivoglio.

CONTENTS

HIGHLIGHTS

A NOTE TO READERS

At Rough Guides, we always strive to bring you the most up-to-date information. This book was produced during a period of continuing uncertainty caused by the Covid-19 pandemic, so please note that content is more subject to change than usual. We recommend checking the latest restrictions and official guidance.

OVERVIEW

La Dotta (The learned). La Grassa (The fat). La Rossa (The red). Stereotypes they may be, but these oft-quoted sobriquets are on the money. Bologna, the capital of Emilia Romagna, is renowned for its university, its cuisine and its traditional left-wing stance. The erudite city is also famous for its beautifully preserved historic centre: a tapestry of medieval streets and squares stitched together by 38 km (24 miles) of porticoes. 'La Rossa' is a nod as much to the rich red of its palaces, towers and colonnaded walkways as it is to the city's left-leaning politics. The main square, Piazza Maggiore, is an open-air museum – a cluster of elegant palazzi crouching beside the imposing Basilica di San Petronio.

Unfurling from the fringes of the Po Plain at the foot of the Apennines, the antique city is a fine example of Roman and medieval town planning, with its ancient town gates, radial plan and long, straight streets. It stands on the Via Emilia, the arrow-straight road laid down by the Romans from Rimini to Piacenza. In the Middle Ages this was where Europe's first university was established, and a town quickly mushroomed around it. Dozens of towers rise above the city, built both as watchtowers and as status symbols by the succession of dynasties that ruled Bologna until it became part of the papal states in 1506. The city prospered from its setting, surrounded by fertile plains and vineyards that supplied its convivial inns. Within its walls, urban life was more liberal than in most other provincial cities, and a free-thinking entrepreneurial people flourished. Today, Bologna is a progressive modern city with a vibrant student population, thriving professional and business sectors, and a buzzing street life.

BOLOGNA LA GRASSA

Of the three nicknames, Bologna is perhaps best known globally as 'La Grassa', a reference to its rich gastronomic tradition. Prosperous

Emilia Romagna is the legendary breadbasket of Italy, a region that has borne foodie delights such as *prosciutto crudo* (Parma ham), Parmesan cheese and balsamic vinegar. Emilian cuisine reaches its height in Bologna, which is widely acclaimed as the culinary capital of Italy. It is famed for its fragrant pink *Mortadella*, *ragù* (the real Bolognese meat sauce) and, above all else, its iconic egg pasta. *Tortellini* alone would be a good enough reason to

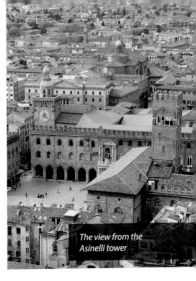

The view from the Asinelli tower

visit Bologna. Legends abound as to the pasta's origins, one of which gives credit to a young cook of a wealthy Bolognese merchant who modelled the pasta on the perfect navel of his master's wife – which, even if apocryphal, says much about the seductiveness of the cuisine. *Sfogline* (someone who makes *sfoglia*; traditionally women) can still be seen rolling out sheets of pasta and cutting the tiny delicate shapes in *trattorias* or through the windows of specialist shops. Flourishing pasta cookery schools (there are 25 in the city) and the annual pasta-making competition, Il Matterello d'Oro (The Golden Rolling Pin), are further evidence that the home-made *tortellini* is in good shape.

A stroll through the twisting medieval streets of the central Mercato di Mezzo reveals enticing food stores and market stalls brimming with fresh produce. Gourmet delis are crammed with whole hanging hams and ginormous wheels of cheese, luring passers-by inside to pick up a few slices of wafer-thin *prosciutto*,

Perfect pasta

The Bolognesi take their food very seriously. In 1972 the Accademia Italiana della Cucina (Academy of Italian Cuisine) decreed that the exact width of a cooked strand of *tagliatelle* must be 1/1,270th of the height of the Asinelli tower, 9mm (0.3 in).

best washed down with a cool glass of Pignoletto. When it comes to restaurants and dining out in the city, it's not so much about Michelin-rosetted temples of cuisine with exotic new delicacies but earthy, family-run *trattorias*, where the recipes are simple and pared-back, and the emphasis is on quality ingredients. While a handful of gourmand places in the city give a nod to lighter contemporary cuisine, Bologna for the most part carries on serving what it's best at – and at a leisurely pace.

CULTURAL LEGACY

The city is as passionate about culture as it is about food, and enjoys a long tradition of intellectual enlightenment. The medieval lawyers, scholars and sculptors of its university paved the way for scientific breakthroughs that helped shape the modern world, and it was the university that was the city's economic powerhouse. The elaborately sculpted sarcophagi of great scholars in the city's Museo Civico Medievale (Medieval Museum) give some idea of the importance attached to academia. Professors rose through the social ranks and were richly rewarded in death as well as life.

The medieval era also witnessed the rise of fine monuments, great Gothic churches rich in art, and the characteristic colonnades. These elegant porticoes, protected as a Unesco World Heritage Site, have always provided a refuge from the elements and a meeting place for Bolognesi from all backgrounds. In times gone by, they provided cover for furtive assassinations and the amorous assignments of, among others, Boccaccio and the Marquis de Sade. Here, Verdi and Rossini trampled the porticoed streets in search of inspiration, just as the late novelist Umberto Eco set out in search of material for his medieval whodunits. Today, during the warmer months, musicians strike up beneath the arcades and artists set up easels. All year round, there is a lively café scene with tables spilling out under the stone arches, assured of shelter from rain, snow or the intense heat of the summer sun.

Thanks to the porticoes and the compact size of the historic centre, Bologna is a delightful city for strolling. A wealth of monuments, museums and artistic treasures calls for several days' exploration. Many of the city's churches are rich repositories of art, while Renaissance or Baroque palazzi – often embellished with frescoes – make fine settings for the city's main museums. Palazzo Poggi, seat of the university, is home to some fascinating specialist museums, while the nearby Pinacoteca houses the city's finest art collection, with works by Giotto, Raphael and the great Bolognese painters. In the Baroque period, the artistic output flourished here, and Bologna became the pre-eminent influence in Italian painting.

Neptune's Fountain

A LIVING CITY

Despite its illustrious history, architectural abundance and gastronomic reputation, Bologna attracts far

Stone porticoes shelter bars and restaurants

fewer tourists than cities such as Florence or Venice. As a result, it feels far more Italian, gritty and real, and less museum-like, offering an enticing alternative to its more popular siblings. Fears of arid scholarship are banished by the buzz of the student area, with bohemian bars overlooking faculties tucked into frescoed palaces. Bolognesi of all ages come out for the evening *passeggiata*, the ritual stroll. There's a vibrant café culture, thriving nightlife, a lively gay scene, and an action-packed calendar of events with concerts, jazz, theatre and art exhibitions. In term time, the population of 390,000 (over 1 million in greater Bologna) swells by around 100,000. But even during the holidays, there's plenty going on, and the Bè Bologna Estate festival from June to September ensures a summer of music, art and theatre. The city has a rich music heritage and has played host to the likes of Verdi, Rossini and Puccini. In 2006, Bologna was appointed Unesco Creative City of Music, a prestigious recognition that honours the city's music tradition – as well as the contemporary scene.

Created on the back of agricultural wealth, the regional economy has flourished for centuries but always moved with the times. Engineering is a regional strength but embraces everything from cutting-edge car manufacture to machine tools and precision robotics. Emilia Romagna is serious car country, with Ferrari, Maserati and Lamborghini all produced here. The city and the region have always been committed to making both money and desirable products, from *Mortadella* cured meat to Ducati motorbikes, while not neglecting agriculture. In keeping with the city's forward-thinking entrepreneurial spirit, manufacturing and the service industries have been decentralized, leaving the historic centre vibrant and liveable yet well preserved.

Contemporary Bologna is not, however, without the social challenges and high unemployment rates that confront other cities of Italy (the Italian youth unemployment rate stands at 28 percent at the time of writing). But this is a city that knows how to thrive, and as the capital of one of the richest regions in Europe, with the

A MEDIEVAL MANHATTAN

In medieval times, Bologna bristled with over 100 towers. Built by Bolognese nobles, these varied in height between 20 metres (65ft) and 60 metres (197ft), with rival families striving to see who could build the highest. But by the sixteenth century, the *torri* had fallen out of fashion. Fire and the fear of collapse were constant hazards, and the great palazzi took over as the main status symbols of noble families. In the late nineteenth century, during urban regeneration, many of the surviving towers were demolished. Most of the remaining ones tend to tilt, often at alarming angles. Alongside the Cattedrale Metropolitana di San Pietro, the poker-straight Azzoguidi tower – also called Altabella (the Tall Beauty) – is the only one standing perfectly vertical. The most famous towers however, and symbols of the city, are the Asinelli and the Garisenda, the 'Twin Towers'. You can climb 498 steps to the top of the Asinelli. Or, if you fancy having a tower all to yourself, book a night's stay in the *Torre Prendiparte* (see page 138). Be warned, though, the price – and the climb to the top – is dizzying.

Inside the ornate Palazzo d'Accursio

third-highest GDP per capita in Italy, it is consistently ranked among the top Italian cities for quality of life. It looks after its cultural legacy too. In recent years, major restoration has spruced up historic monuments within the city centre. A cluster of buildings – mainly churches and palaces – has been recovered by the Fondazione Cassa di Risparmio and now forms part of a cultural itinerary for visitors. A further incentive for visitors is the city's location at a major rail hub, making it the perfect springboard for day-trips to the art-filled cities scattered throughout Emilia Romagna. A mere half-hour train journey takes you to Modena, the birthplace of one Pavarotti, and the home of Maserati and Ferrari, as well as of a superlative Duomo. Gourmet Parma is less than an hour away. Closer to Bologna, the Colli Bolognesi – the first foothills of the verdant Apennines – provide welcome respite from the sweltering city streets in summer.

Bologna has many facets: a city of history, expressed in every tower and portico; a city of culture, brimming with museums and the inspiration for musicians and artists; a leading university city; a city of gastronomy; and a city of business and trade. But, above all, this is a city where everything is harmonious, and the cult of beauty permeates most aspects of life. 'La Rossa' notwithstanding, Bologna remains a paradigm of the good life: a citadel of good taste set in the proverbial land of plenty.

HISTORY AND CULTURE

Bologna's location, strategically sited between northern and central-southern Italy, has been both a curse and a blessing for the city. The Bolognesi haven't enjoyed many centuries of peace but the various powers that coveted and ruled over the centuries left behind a heady mix of culture and riches. Despite invasions, sieges and plagues, as well as devastation in World War II, Bologna has managed to emerge as one of Italy's wealthiest and most dynamic cities. Its history goes back to a pre-Etruscan civilization, but it is the medieval period, when a russet redbrick turreted town grew up around Europe's oldest university, that truly defines the city.

Carving depicting early students at the university

EARLY SETTLERS

As the Bronze Age merged into the Iron Age in around the ninth century BC, northern and central Italy were occupied by the Villanovian civilization, named after a site discovered at Villanova just outside Bologna in 1859. This gave way in the sixth century to an Etruscan settlement, called Felsina, on the area where Bologna is today. The town flourished as a trading centre thanks to its link to the port of Spina on the Po Delta. It was a period of peace and prosperity, and by the eighth century, the Etruscans were dominating the entire region. Displays in Bologna's Archaeological Museum, including grave goods, exquisite statuettes and jewellery, give an insight into the affluence and sophistication of the Etruscan culture.

At the start of the fourth century, Etruscan Bologna underwent radical upheaval, with successive waves of invasions by the Celts from over the Alps. The Celtic peoples occupied large stretches of Italy, north of the Apennines and the Marches region. It was the Boii people who gave the name Bononia to the settlement when it came under Roman control in 189 BC. By this time, the Romans had conquered Cisalpine Gaul and set up colonies in the fertile Po Plain. They had built the Via Flaminia, stretching from the Adriatic coast over the Apennines to Rome, and in 187 BC completed the long

Bologna's Two Towers

straight Via Aemilia (Emilia), running from Rimini on the east coast to Piacenza, through their newly conquered territories. This established Bononia as a key centre, linking up with the Via Flaminia and hence giving direct military and trading access from Rome. The settlement was substantially rebuilt and extended and, although much of Roman Bologna is overlaid by the medieval city, Roman street plans are still visible and the route of the old Via Emilia cuts right through the centre. There are also Roman remains in the Archaeological Museum and in churches where Roman capitals were recycled and incorporated into medieval columns in surprisingly harmonious ways.

HUNS, GOTHS AND LOMBARDS

In the early fifth century, the region fell prey to barbaric invaders emigrating south, with invasions from Visigoths and Huns. Despite the incursions, a strong Roman Christian culture prevailed. The close relationship between Ambrogio, the Archbishop of Milan, and the Bolognese Bishop, Petronius, who later became the patron saint of the city, enabled the construction of the first wall around the city and the addition of 'holy protection' in the form of four crosses set outside the walls.

Ravenna, a relatively unknown provincial town surrounded by swampland, took centre stage when Honorius, last Emperor of Rome, made it capital of the Western Roman Empire in 404. With the fall of the Western Roman Empire in 476, it came under Gothic rule, like the rest of Italy, but enjoyed a period of recovery and became a rich and powerful city, famous for its glittering early Christian and Byzantine mosaics.

The Lombard King Liutprand captured Bologna in 727. Less than 50 years later, the Lombards in turn were ousted by the Franks under Charlemagne who restored the city to the papacy. The city's most ancient churches date back to this era.

Porticoes of Via Farini

COMMUNES AND DYNASTIC POWERS

In the eleventh and twelfth centuries, Bologna succeeded in wresting itself from Ravenna, whose archbishops controlled the region. It was now free to enjoy the status of an independent commune – or free city state, thus ensuring considerable political and economic autonomy. The University of Bologna, which is now recognized as the oldest in Europe, was founded in 1088 and brought international renown to the city (see box, opposite). It was a period of major development too, with the creation of elegant porticoes and high-rise towers, built for wealthy families. Less evident today are the canals which served the watermills to power the textile industries, especially silk. The waterways were also used for ships carrying cargo as trade expanded. By 1200, Bologna had a population of around 50,000 and was one of the great cities of Europe.

But, as in the rest of Italy, it was also a time of factional strife. The city was one of the main cities of the Lombard League (1167), a medieval alliance of North Italian communes against Emperor Frederick I Barbarossa. There were constant struggles between the Guelphs, supporters of the free cities and the pope, and the pro-Holy Roman Empire Ghibellines. The Guelphs fought constantly with Ghibelline Modena and won a victory against them at the Battle of Fossalta in 1249. The son of Emperor Frederick II, known as Enzo of Sardinia, was captured and imprisoned in Bologna's Palazzo di Re Enzo until his death in 1273.

Internal power struggles led to the decline of the communes and the rise of the region's great family dynasties, ranging from semi-feudal lordships to fully fledged dukedoms and courts of European renown. Throughout the fifteenth century, Bologna was governed by the mighty Bentivoglio family, who produced five successive leaders, and introduced an enlightened regime, bringing in the printing press and embarking on a building programme.

Dynastic rule was elevated to a way of life, with the noble courts becoming noted centres of culture, from the Farnese dynasty in

BOLOGNA 'LA DOTTA' (THE LEARNED)

Medieval Bologna's most significant event was the foundation of Europe's first university, believed to have been in 1088. For the first 470 or so years of its existence, the university had no fixed location and lectures were held in public buildings or convent halls scattered around the city. Under Pius IV, the Palazzo dell'Archiginnasio (see page 38) was built in the city centre in 1562 and this served as the seat of the university until 1803 when it moved permanently to its present premises on Via Zamboni. The prestige of the law school made the city a European centre of scholarship which drew the finest minds of the day. Bologna also developed one of Europe's earliest medical schools and acquired a reputation for scientific research that survives to this day. Palazzo Poggi, the present-day seat of the university, is home to many of its faculties, the university library and a cluster of museums, including some fascinating scientific collections that were used for teaching in former times. The university remains one of the country's finest academic institutions and boasts some of the loveliest university buildings in the country.

Statue of Pope Gregory XIII, University of Bologna

Parma to the d'Este dukes in Ferrara, and the Malatesta lords in Rimini. During the Renaissance, the ducal courts, especially those of the d'Este, became artistic centres attracting the finest talent.

CENTURIES OF PAPAL DOMINATION

Bologna's role as a prestigious centre of learning had helped make the city one of the richest, most important and densely populated in Europe. Such prosperity and independence presented a threat to papal power, so the city was annexed by the Papal States in 1506 when Pope Julius besieged Bologna. A year later, encouraged by the papacy, the Bolognesi sacked the monumental palace of the now fallen-from-favour Bentivoglios. Parma and Piacenza were later annexed by the Papal States, and the papal dynasty ended one of the most enlightened Renaissance city-states when it swallowed up Ferrara in 1598, and the remains of the d'Este dukedom were transferred to Modena.

The life of Bologna as part of the Papal States was to endure for almost three centuries. When Charles V was crowned Holy Roman Emperor by the pope in 1530, he chose to have the coronation in Bologna's Basilica di San Petronio. His troops had sacked Rome three years earlier, and Bologna by this stage enjoyed an importance second only to the capital of the Papal States. It was a double coronation, for Charles was also crowned King of Italy in the Palazzo Pubblico (now the Palazzo Comunale). The combined event was chronicled as the 'Triumph of Bologna' for the pomp and splendour of the ceremonies. The following few months saw fervent construction in the city: the papacy showcasing its power through symbolic triumphal arches, classical architecture and statues.

The last decades of the sixteenth century saw the school of Bolognese painters flourish under the Carraccis, the family of artists who challenged the affectations of Mannerism and satisfied the desire of the Counter-Reformation for a new religious art of simplicity and clarity with a direct appeal to the emotions. Guido Reni, who trained with the Carracci, became one of the greatest painters of the seventeenth century. But while Bologna was a major art centre and this period saw a rise of new churches, monasteries and palazzi, it was otherwise a time of political and intellectual stagnation, dominated by the reactionary reforms of the Counter-Reformation.

FOREIGN INTERVENTION

Papal rule was interrupted briefly when Napoleonic troops swept into Italy in 1796. Bologna, Ferrara, Mantua and Reggio Emilia formed the Cispadane Republic, later to be amalgamated in to the short-lived Cisalpine Republic with Milan as its capital. The French, who were welcomed in Bologna, made improvements to the city, such as the ring road outside the city walls and the transfer of the University from the Archiginnasio to Palazzo Poggi.

Under the Congress of Vienna in 1815, following the defeat of Napoleon, Bologna was returned to the Papal States. But real control of much of northern Italy rested with reactionary Austria, whose troops garrisoned the city from 1815. Insurrections spread through Bologna, Modena and Parma, starting in 1831. Austrian rule finally came to an end when Camillo Cavour, the architect of Italian Unification, decided the only way of defeating Austria was with the support of France. In 1859, the troops of Vittorio Emanuele and Napoleon III of France defeated the Austrians at Magenta and Solferino. The following year, the citizens of Bologna voted to become part of the Kingdom of Savoy, which was to become the Kingdom of Italy in 1861.

WORLD WAR II

The nineteenth century saw Bologna rehearsing its future role as a radical socialist city in a left-leaning region within the broad 'red belt' of central Italy. Even so, the city flirted with Fascism during the period between the two world wars, and paid the price in 1943–5. The Emilian Apennines marked the Nazis' Gothic Line, making Bologna a strategic target for Allied attacks. The aerial bombardments wreaked havoc on the city, destroying or severely damaging over 40 percent of the buildings in the historic centre.

The bourgeoisie and the land-owning classes succumbed to Fascism, but during the last days of the war, partisans from the area provided the fiercest resistance to Nazi occupation. The Bologna hinterland also suffered Italy's worst Nazi atrocity against civilians. In 1944, the Marzabotto massacre of 1830 civilians and partisans in the Apennines, south of Bologna, spurred widespread condemnation, as did the Nazi deportation of Jews from Ferrara and Bologna.

MODERN BOLOGNA

In 1945, the city elected a Communist administration and never really looked back. The administration mutated into a left-wing coalition and, over the next 50 years, imposed an individualistic, modern vision on the city. Bologna became one of the first cities to show that there was no contradiction between a left-wing council and capitalism with a human face. It privatized key social services and encouraged public-private partnership. A bastion of social democracy, civil rights and communal culture, the city pioneered pedestrian precincts, conservation areas, communal housing, gay rights and affordable childcare, as well as sheltered housing for the elderly and student facilities.

Engraved portrait of Camillo Cavour, leading figure in Italian Unification movement

But the city of good governance was not without its fair share of the turbulence rippling throughout the rest of Italy during the late 1960s and 1970s. Over a decade of political crime and violent clashes culminated in the 'Bologna Massacre' on 2 August 1980, when a bomb attributed to a Fascist terrorist organization ripped through a Central Station waiting room, killing 85 and wounding 200. A gash in the wall and the station clock, permanently fixed at 10.25am, the exact time of the explosion, commemorate the event.

To the dismay of local leftists, the long line of left-wing mayors was broken when a centre-right coalition, headed by conservative businessman Giorgio Guazzaloca, won the elections in 1999. In 2004, the left came back to power and has kept it ever since. Centre-left Flavio Delbono resigned after seven months at his post following his involvement in a corruption scandal, and was replaced by Virginio

The Fiera, one of Europe's largest exhibition centres

Merola in 2011. In 2021, centre-left Matteo Lepore was elected mayor, ending Merola's two-term tenure, and has since showed signs of progressive leadership. He signed Bologna up for the European Commission's 100 Climate-Neutral and Smart Cities, a scheme to dramatically reduce emissions by 2030. One of his most innovative drives was to pioneer a 2022 law that, if successful, will grant honorary citizenship to children born in Italy to foreign parents – a forward-thinking move in a country where anti-immigration populist parties have proliferated in recent years.

Bologna has a thriving industrial sector, with emphasis on engineering, electronics, machinery and automobiles. The Fiera is one of Europe's largest exhibition centres, hosting around 30 annual international events – from construction to cosmetics. Like the rest of the country, Bologna has suffered from the economic downturn in recent years, only exacerbated by the Covid-19 pandemic. As the first major western country to be hit by the virus, the impact on Italy was extreme, and despite swift government action and a severe lockdown, death rates were high. For a country that relies on tourism, the economic impact has been acute, slashing GDP generated by the travel industry in half in 2020. However, 2022 is showing signs of recovery, with tourist traffic on the rise, and the fact that many hotels, restaurants and shops are family-owned may have contributed to the fact that relatively few in Bologna (and the rest of the country) have closed down.

IMPORTANT DATES

9th century BC Villanovan civilization emerges near Bologna.
4–5th century BC Etruscan settlements in Felsina (Bologna).
189 BC Foundation of Roman Bologna (called Bononia)
AD 402 Ravenna proclaimed capital of the Western Roman Empire.
476 Ravenna conquered, signalling the fall of the Western Roman Empire
751 End of Byzantine domination in northern Italy.
1088 Foundation of Bologna University, the oldest in Europe.
1374 Bologna's city walls completed.
1460–1506 Bologna ruled by the local Bentivoglio lords.
1506 Bologna annexed by the Papal States.
1629–31 Bologna loses 15,000 citizens in the plague of 1629–31.
1797–1802 The city becomes part of the Napoleonic Cisalpine Republic.
1815 Bologna and Emilia restored to the Papal States.
1871 Italian Unification.
1915 Italy joins the World War I Allies.
1940 Italy enters World War II as an ally of Nazi Germany.
1943–5 Bologna bombed by the Allies.
1945–9 Bologna has an uninterrupted string of left-wing mayors.
1980 Fascist terror attack on Bologna Central Station, with 85 deaths.
1982 Italian football team wins World Cup in Spain.
2000 Bologna is European Capital of Culture.
2006 Bologna is named Unesco City of Music.
2010 Centre-left mayor, Flavio Delbono, resigns after corruption scandals.
2011 Virginio Merola elected as mayor, leads a left-wing coalition.
2012 Earthquake in Emilia-Romagna leave 26 dead, 20,000 homeless.
2016 900th anniversary of the founding of the city.
2018 Giuseppe Conte (independent) becomes Italian prime minister. A hung parliament results in an uneasy coalition between two anti-establishment parties: Lega and Five Star Movement.
2020 Covid-19 sweeps Italy and the rest of the world, devastating tourism.
2021 Centre-left Matteo Lepore elected mayor.
2022 Travel starts to pick up again, with tourists to Italy on the rise.

Fontana del Nettuno

OUT AND ABOUT

Bologna, with its labyrinthine streets, forgotten chapels and imposing temples to scholarship, is ripe for exploration on foot. Almost all the cultural attractions are packed into the historic centre, a large part of which has traffic restrictions from 7am to 8pm. Furthermore, the city is flat, and the pavements are protected from the elements by the colonnaded porticos. From Piazza Maggiore and the famous two towers, a web of streets fans out towards the city gates and the *viali*, the circle of avenues tracing the ancient walls. Via dell'Indipendenza links the rail and bus stations to Piazza Maggiore, and, at its southern end, forms a T with Via Ugo Bassi running west and Via Rizzo running east. These three main arteries, which are Bologna's high streets, are completely car-free at weekends.

PIAZZA MAGGIORE AND AROUND

Piazza Maggiore and its antechamber, Piazza del Nettuno, form the symbolic heart of the city, showcasing the political and religious institutions that define independent-minded Bologna. Overlooked by brick-built palazzi and the vast mass of San Petronio, the sweeping Piazza Maggiore was – and to a certain extent still is – the stage for Bolognesi speeches, ceremonies, meetings and protests. Just off the piazza, the maze-like food market provides culinary diversion, and the porticoes shelter some of the city's most exclusive shops.

PIAZZA DEL NETTUNO

The ringmaster to the performance of daily life on the square is a monumental, muscle-bound Neptune. A popular meeting

The Neptune Maserati link

Motoring enthusiasts may recognize Neptune's trident in the *Fontana del Nettuno*. It was adopted by the Modena-based Maserati car company as their logo.

place for the Bolognesi, the **Fontana del Nettuno** ❶ was sculpted by Giambologna in 1556. An Italian in all but birth (he was born Jean Boulogne in Flanders), the Mannerist sculptor spent most of his working life in Florence, but it was the Fountain of Neptune in Bologna that cemented his reputation. The bronze sculpture depicts an immense Neptune (nicknamed 'Il Gigante') with four *putti,* representing the winds, and four voluptuous sirens sitting astride dolphins, spouting water from their nipples. Given Bologna's turbulent relationship with the papacy, citizens delighted in the fact that the nude Neptune was considered a profane, pagan symbol by the papal authorities. The statue caused a furore when first unveiled, and a Counter-Reformation edict decreed that Neptune should be robed. But the priapic sea god is now free to frolic. Locals take great delight in pointing out the best vantage point for viewing the god's impressive manhood.

PALAZZO RE ENZO AND PALAZZO DEL PODESTÀ

Squaring up to the fountain, from the east side of the square, is **Palazzo Re Enzo** (access only during exhibitions), named after the son of Emperor Frederick II, Enzo 'King of Sardinia', who was defeated at the Guelphs versus Ghibellines Battle of Fossalta in 1249 and was imprisoned here for 23 years, until his death in 1272. Huddled up to the palace and facing Piazza Maggiore is the handsome **Palazzo del Podestà** (access only during exhibitions), built as the political seat of power in the thirteenth century. It is graced by a Renaissance porticoed facade on the Piazza Maggiore side and distinguished by its thirteenth-century brick tower, the

Torre dell'Arengo, originally built to summon citizens in case of emergency. The vault below, the Voltone del Podesta, was once occupied by terracotta statues of the town's patron saints. The attraction today is the echo in the 'whispering gallery' – face one of the four corners of the arcade and your voice will murmur back to you from the opposite corner.

The wall on the west side of Piazza del Nettuno features photos of hundreds of partisans who fought for the Resistance in World War II. Of the 14,425 local partisans, including over 2000 women, 2059 died. Italy was liberated from Nazi domination on 21 April 1945, by which time Bologna had been devastated by aerial bombardments. A further memorial honours the victims of the bomb explosion at Bologna's main railway station in 1980, which left 85 dead and 200 wounded.

PALAZZO D'ACCURSIO

The imposing building looming above the western flank of Piazza Maggiore is the **Palazzo d'Accursio**, also known as the **Palazzo Comunale** ❷ (www.musei-bologna.it/arteantica; Tues–Sun 9am–6.30pm, some ceremonial halls open Tues–Sun 10am–1pm if not being used for council meetings; charge only for the Collezioni Comunali d'Arte, the Municipal Art Collection). The palace dates back to the thirteenth

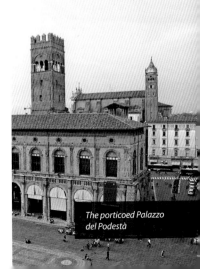

The porticoed Palazzo del Podestà

century and was originally the residence of a well-known medieval lawyer, Accursius. It was later bought by the city and remodelled as an affirmation of papal authority. In 1530, two days before he was crowned Emperor in San Petronio, Charles V was crowned King of Italy in the chapel of the Palazzo d'Accursio, receiving the Iron Cross of Lombardy. A suspended passageway was built especially for the occasion, linking the palace to San Petronio across Piazza Maggiore.

The huge bronze statue (1580) above the portal of the palace depicts Pope Gregory XIII, the Bolognese pope who reformed the old Roman calendar, replacing it with his own Gregorian one, still in use today. Above and to the left of the doorway is a beautiful terracotta statue of the *Virgin and Child* (1478) by the Italian sculptor Niccolò dell'Arca. Cross the courtyard and climb the magnificent corded staircases, where horses once thundered past, to the frescoed interiors on the first and second floors. Restyled by papal legates in the sixteenth century, the **ceremonial halls** are elaborately frescoed and have fine views over the square. The Sala Rossa, or Red Room, with its huge chandeliers, is a favourite venue for civil ceremonies. The Museo Morandi, which opened here in 1993, was moved to MAMbo (see page 64) in 2012 while this part of the palace was restored.

Palazzo Comunale

The museum will return here after the work is complete, though no date has yet been set. The many rooms of the **Collezioni Comunali d'Art** at the top of the palace display Emilian works of art from the thirteenth to nineteenth centuries, worth visiting for a sense of the decor, furnishings and artistic taste under papal rule, rather than for great art.

SALABORSA

Part of the monumental Palazzo Comunale complex, the **Biblioteca Salaborsa** (www,bibliotecasalaborsa.it; Mon–Fri 2–7pm; free) was built within the shell of the former Stock Exchange (Borsa). The building is now a spacious multimedia library and cultural space, designed in Art Nouveau style. A glass floor in the Covered Square reveals excavations of the medieval and Roman settlements, including part of the forum and Roman pavement, and these can be accessed from the lower basement level.

Before its current role, this sizeable section of the Palazzo Comunale served diverse purposes. In 1568, the Bolognese naturalist, Ulisse Aldrovandi, founded Bologna's botanic garden – one of Europe's first – in the courtyard here for the academic study of medicinal plants (the city's botanic garden today is in the university quarter). The courtyard later became a training ground for the military, then in the twentieth century served variously as bank offices, a puppet theatre and a basketball ground before becoming the Stock Exchange.

PIAZZA MAGGIORE

A sunny day is a summons to sit at café tables in the **Piazza Maggiore** ❸ or on the steps beneath the arcades and soak up the atmosphere. Dominating the great central square is the hulking (but incomplete) Basilica di San Petronio – favourite church of the Bolognesi. The raised platform in the middle of the piazza

Bologna Welcome Card

The excellent tourist office on Piazza Maggiore can supply you with a Bologna Welcome Card. At €25 for the Bologna Welcome Card Easy and €40 for the Bologna Welcome Card Plus, they are good value, giving you free admission to many city museums and attractions, plus discounts for shops, restaurants and events. Also available at www. bolognawelcome.com.

is familiarly called the *crescentone* after the name of the local flat bread, *crescente*, which it resembles in shape.

BASILICA DI SAN PETRONIO

Dedicated to Petronius, the city's patron saint, the hulking great fourteenth-century **Basilica di San Petronio ❹** (www.basilicadisanpetronio. org; daily 8.30am–1.30pm & 3–6.30pm; church: free, terrace: charge) is the city's principal church. As one of the most monumental Gothic basilicas in Italy, the church would have been larger than St Peter's in Rome had not Pope Pius IV put a stop to construction by using the funds for the creation of a new university, the Palazzo Archiginnasio. As a consequence, the facade was never completed, hence only the partial cladding in pink Verona marble and the cut-off transept, which you can see down the alley to the right of the basilica. Even so, San Petronio is still formidable, representing a manifestation of civic will rather than religious power. Built over Roman foundations, the vaulted church reveals columns recycled from the Augustan era, which meld perfectly with medieval additions.

The highly expressive reliefs on the **Porta Magna**, the central portal, were the last great work of Sienese sculptor Jacopo della Quercia, occupying the last 13 years of his life (1425–38). The architrave is etched with scenes from the New Testament, and on the two pilasters on either side of the door, dramatic reliefs with subjects taken from the Old Testament. Michelangelo, who visited Bologna in 1494, admired these reliefs and used several of the motifs (such as *The Creation of Adam*) for the Sistine Chapel ceiling. The lunette features the *Madonna and Child* between St Petronius and St Ambrose.

The immense but simple interior of the basilica has witnessed historical events, not least of which was the crowning of Charles V as Holy Roman Emperor in 1530 (see page 23). Set in the floor on the left is a seventeenth-century sundial, measuring almost 60m (197ft) and said to be the world's biggest church sundial. It was of particular interest to travellers on the Grand Tour and, today, it still attracts plenty of interest, especially at noon on a sunny day when rays touch the line of the sundial. The second chapel on the left is dedicated to San Petronio and contains the relics of the saint. The

San Petronio's half-completed facade

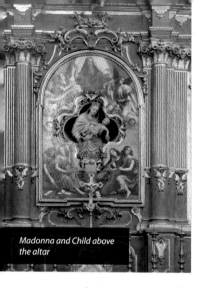

Madonna and Child above the altar

Bolognini Chapel (fourth on the left) remains virtually intact, and has striking early fifteenth-century frescoes by Giovanni da Modena, depicting the *Journey of the Magi, the Life of St Petronius, Paradise* and a harrowing scene of the *Last Judgement*. There are 20 more chapels, an organ to the right of the altar, dating from 1470 and still functioning (the one opposite still works, too, but is relatively modern at 1596), and a museum with projects for the completion of the facade which were never carried through.

Make a beeline for the **panoramic terrace** crowning the basilica (access from Piazza Galvani by lift and a few steps; Sat & holidays only 10am–1pm & 3–6.30pm, Fri–Sun 10am–1pm & 2.30–6pm) for splendid views of the cityscape and, beyond, the Apennine hills undulating south.

MUSEO CIVICO ARCHEOLOGICO

From Piazza Maggiore, the Via dell'Archiginnasio takes you beneath the porticoes past the city's most elegant shops, including the loveliest arcades, known as the Pavaglione. The **Museo Civico Archeologico** **5** (www.museibologna.it/archeologico; Mon & Wed–Fri 9am–2pm, Thurs 3–7pm, Fri–Sun 10am–7pm; opening times may be extended during temporary exhibitions) is housed in the former hospital of Santa Maria della Morte (of Death), which was dedicated to the terminally ill. The lovely courtyard is framed by Roman statuary and leads to Giambologna's statue of Neptune, displayed at the top of the main staircase. Bologna's early history is traced through Celtic tools, Etruscan urns, Attic vases and Classical Greek terracottas, proof that the Bolognese talent for trading dates back to its earliest history. The sheer number of exhibits – around 200,000 – in old-fashioned, dimly lit galleries can be overwhelming, but the museum has one of the best Etruscan collections in Italy. Two large galleries are devoted to the Etruscan civilization in Bologna (ninth to fourth centuries BC), featuring terracotta and bronze ossuaries, funerary stelae with depictions of fantastic animals, and exquisite terracotta askos (small vessels for pouring liquids). There are also good displays

CITY OF PORTICOES

A distinctive feature of the city are the *portici*, or porticoes, stretching for almost 40km (25 miles) through the historic core. These graceful, tranquil arcades were originally built of wood outside shopkeepers' houses as extra space for trade. The original portico had to be a minimum of 7 'Bolognese feet' high (2.66m) to enable those on horseback to pass through. From 1568, due mainly to fire hazards, porticoes had to be made of brick or stone. A few of the old wooden ones survive, and one of the best-preserved examples is the lofty portico of Casa Isolani in Strada Maggiore. The Portico San Luca, running for nearly 3.5km (2 miles) up to the hilltop Sanctuary of San Luca, is the longest portico in the world. Over the centuries, the porticoes have been much admired by travellers both for their architectural interest and their protection against the elements. In a city renowned for rain and snow in winter, and searing heat in midsummer, they couldn't be more convenient.

of Roman antiquities and (easy to miss) an impressive Egyptian collection in the basement.

PALAZZO DELL'ARCHIGINNASIO

Just beyond the Archeological Museum is the cultural set-piece of the frescoed **Palazzo dell'Archiginnasio ❻**, built in 1562–3 as the first permanent seat of Europe's most ancient university (www.archiginnasio.it; Palace Courtyard and open gallery: Mon–Fri 10am–6pm, Sat 10am–7pm, Sun 10am–2pm, free; Anatomical Theatre and Stabat Mater Hall: Mon–Fri 10am–6pm, Sat 10am–7pm, Sun & hols 10am–2pm, if not occupied by events; hours vary in winter, check website). Before the construction of the Archiginnasio, the schools of law and medicine had been scattered around various venues of the city. This remained the seat of the university until 1803, when it moved to its current location in Via Zamboni. Today, the palace houses the precious collection of 800,000 works of the Biblioteca Comunale (City Library), the richly decorated Sala dello Stabat Mater, a former lecture hall where Rossini's first Italian performance of *Stabat Mater* was held in 1842 under the direction of Donizetti, and the fascinating Teatro Anatomico (Anatomy Theatre).

The fine courtyard, with its double loggia, and the staircase and halls are all decorated by memorials commemorating academic masters, together with around 6,000 student coats of arms. The courtyard was frequently the scene of scholarly ceremonies, one of the most intriguing being the Preparation of the Teriaca (Theriac), a drug for animal bites and later the all-cure medicine, formulated by the Greeks in the first century AD and concocted from fermented herbs, poisons, animal flesh, honey and numerous other ingredients.

Some of the first human dissections in Europe were performed in the **Teatro Anatomico**, shaped like an amphitheatre and adorned with wooden statues of famous university anatomists and celebrated doctors. There is nothing remotely macabre about the tiered seats and professors' chair – apart from a canopy supported by depictions of a couple of skinned cadavers, *gli spellati*. The Church forbade regular sessions of dissections but when they did take place, they were popular events, open to the public. As photos at the entrance illustrate, this wing of the building was devastated during the bombardment of 1944, but was reconstructed immediately after the war, using the original wooden sculptures that were salvaged from the rubble.

The Via dell'Archiginnasio leads into **Piazza Galvani**, named after the eighteenth-century Bolognese scientist Luigi Galvani, pioneer of bioelectromagnetics. Through his experiments on frogs, he established that bioelectric forces exist within animal tissue. The statue in the square shows Galvani gazing at a frog on a stone slab. For a break from sightseeing, swing by *Caffè Zanarini* on the corner of the piazza, a great spot for coffee and cakes.

QUADRILATERO

The maze of alleys tucked away off Piazza Maggiore is known as the Quadrilatero. It is an ancient grid of food shops, where the mood is as boisterous as it was in its medieval heyday. The ancient guilds of the city, such as goldsmiths,

Tamburini deli

blacksmiths, butchers, fishmongers and furriers, had their head-quarters here; many of the street names today recall their trades. The market is the place for a true taste of Emilia, with open-air stalls, specialist food shops and a covered market, **Mercato di Mezzo ❼**, now repurposed as a stylish food hall selling enticing regional produce and freshly made tapas-style snacks to take away or eat in, very casually, at communal tables. From here, the market spills out onto Via Drapperie, Via Clavature and Via degli Orefici. Gaze and graze is the mantra of most visitors. Pick from juicy peaches and cherries, sculpted pastries, navel-shaped handmade pasta, slivers of delicious pink Parma ham, succulent Bolognese *Mortadella*, still-wriggling seafood and wedges of superior 'black rind' parmesan.

By day, few people can resist lunch at **Tamburini** (Via Drapperie/Via Caprarie 1), the legendary gourmet deli with a self-service food bar, followed perhaps by a delicious pastry at **Atti** (Via Drapperie 6); or a picnic of charcuterie from **Salumeria Simoni** (Via Drapperie

WHERE TIME STANDS STILL

Only the word 'Vino' above the doorway hints that you might have arrived at an inn. The inconspicuous *Osteria del Sole*, just off Via Pescheria at Vicolo Ranocchi 1D (www.osteriadelsole.it), is Bologna's oldest inn, dating from 1465. It's an atmospheric, rough-and-ready spot, with old framed photos on the walls, cheap wine served by the glass, and long tables for customers to bring their own food – which they have done for centuries. Pick up charcuterie from the market stalls or from neighbouring delis, order your glass of Sangiovese or Pignoletto, and sit with cheerful old boys playing cards, students from the university or the occasional in-the-know tourist who has managed to locate this elusive inn.

Lamentation over the Dead Christ

5/2A), where whole hams hang from the ceiling and wheels of cheeses and thick rolls of *Mortadella* are crammed into the windows. In the evening, the Quadrilatero becomes a chic spot for an *aperitivo* in an outdoor café.

SANTA MARIA DELLA VITA

After the bustle of the surrounding market, the church of **Santa Maria della Vita** ❽ (Via Clavature 8; www.genusbononiae.it; Tues–Sun 10am–7pm) is a haven of peace. Although boldly frescoed, the restored Baroque interior is overshadowed by the *Lamentation over the Dead Christ* (1463) by Niccolò dell'Arca, a remarkable composition in terracotta portraying life-size grieving mourners at the death of Christ. The church was part of a religious hospital complex, and it is thought that Niccolò dell'Arca may well have studied the faces of the sick and suffering to have achieved such stunningly raw expressions of grief. The figure of Nicodemus is traditionally described as a self-portrait. In the oratory, where temporary exhibitions are often held, there is another poignant lament in terracotta, the *Death of the Virgin*, by Alfonso Lombardi.

EAST OF PIAZZA MAGGIORE

With its long rows of noble palazzi and secret courtyards, the east side of the medieval city has always been the most fashionable quarter of the city. The Strada Maggiore traces the route of the Roman Via Emilia which linked with the Via Flaminia – the road to Rome. The porticoed street is lined by a string of senatorial palazzi, which once belonged to ruling families. To the north, Via San Vitale was formerly called Via Salaria, for it was along here that salt was carted into the city from the Cervia salt flats south of Ravenna. Via Santo Stefano, the ancient road to Tuscany, is flanked by yet more fine mansions and leads to, and beyond, the beguiling complex of Santo Stefano.

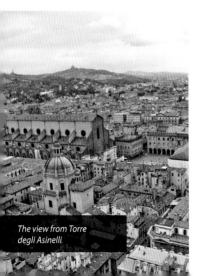

The view from Torre degli Asinelli

DUE TORRI

Dominating Piazza di Porta Ravegnana, site of the main gate of the Roman walls, are the **Due Torri** ❾, the iconic Two Towers. The **Torre degli Asinelli** (www.duetorribologna.com; daily 10am–5pm (timeslots every 15 min;

booking essential) and the **Torre Garisenda** (no access) are the most potent symbols of the medieval era, when Bologna bristled with around 120 towers. Both date back to the twelfth century, and were probably built as watchtowers as well as status symbols. Legend has it that the two richest families in Bologna, the Asinelli and the Garisenda, competed to build the tallest and most beautiful tower in the city.

A sense of history and a bird's-eye view over the terracotta rooftops should tempt you to the top of Torre degli Asinelli (over 97m/318ft). It is admittedly a vertiginous climb, with a narrow spiral staircase of 498 steps, but worth the effort. From the top, you can spot some of the other 20-odd surviving medieval towers and, on a clear day, the foothills of the Alps beyond Verona. Like most of Bologna's towers, the Due Torri are both tilting: Garisenda 3.33m (11ft) to the northeast, Asinelli 2.23m (7.3ft) to the west. Garisenda originally rose to 60m (197ft) but it was built on weak foundations, and for safety reasons 12m (39ft) was lopped off in the mid-fourteenth century. From certain angles, however, the twin landmarks appear to be the same height. Dante, who was briefly in Bologna during his exile from Florence, and saw the acutely tilting tower (before it was shortened), included it in *The Inferno*, where he compares it to the bending Antaeus, giant son of Poseidon, frozen in ice at the bottom of hell. His quote is engraved on a plaque at the base of the tower.

Squatting in the shadow of the towers, but in no way inconspicuous, is the seventeenth-century church of **San Bartolomeo**, with a Renaissance portico. Look for the *Annunciation* by Francesco Albani in the fourth chapel of the south aisle, and the small *Madonna with Child* by Guido Reni in the north transept. On the north side of the square, the intrusion of a starkly modern office building invariably sparked a public outcry when constructed in the 1950s.

Tilting towers

In 1786, the German writer Goethe, in an unusually flippant mood, got the measure of the Bolognese nobility: "Building a tower became both a hobby and a point of honour. In time, perpendicular towers became commonplace, so everyone wanted a leaning one."

PIAZZA DELLA MERCANZIA

Core of the commercial district since medieval times, **Piazza della Mercanzia ⑩** is dominated by the crenellated **Palazzo della Mercanzia**, formerly the merchants' exchange and customs house, now seat of Bologna's Chamber of Commerce. The Gothic facade is adorned by statues representing the city's patron saints who smile benignly on an economy once based on gold, textiles, silk and hemp, but now in thrall to local success stories such as pricey La Perla lingerie, hemp-free Bruno Magli shoes and Mandarina Duck bags. The palace safeguards the original recipes of local specialities, such as *tagliatelle al ragù* (with the real Bolognese sauce). *Pappagallo* (see page 109), a charming old-world institution in a beautiful thirteenth-century building on the piazza, is a good place to try it.

STRADA MAGGIORE

Running southeast from Piazza Mercanzia is **Strada Maggiore** or Main Street, with an almost uninterrupted succession of aristocratic residences. On the left-hand side, at No 26, is the **Casa Rossini ⑪**, the composer's home from 1829 and 1848. Just beyond it, on the right, is the lofty and quaintly porticoed **Casa Isolani**, one of the city's few surviving thirteenth-century houses. Beyond, the **Caffè Commercianti** (No 23c) is the favoured haunt of the academic set, including the late polymath and best-selling author,

Umberto Eco. Modelled on a Parisian café, it has Art Deco and Art Nouveau touches, and makes a chic coffee or cocktail stop.

MUSEO INTERNAZIONALE E BIBLIOTECA DELLA MUSICA

A mere baton's throw from Rossini's home, the Palazzo Sanguinetti at No 34 Strada Maggiore is home to the delightful **Museo Internazionale e Biblioteca della Musica** ⓬ (International Museum and Library of Music; www.museibologna.it/musica; Tues–Fri 11am–1.30pm & 2.30–6.30pm, Sat & Sun 10am–7pm). Rossini and his second wife, Olympe Pélissier, were hosted here by their tenor friend, Domenico Donzelli. The museum is a recognition of Bologna's musical status: nine rooms trace six centuries of European music through 80 rare and antique musical instruments, along with scores, historical documents and portraits. Even those who are not fans of classical music will be entranced by the *trompe-l'œil* courtyard and the frescoed interiors, offering a rare glimpse into how the Bolognese nobility lived. The salon-like atmosphere, reflected in the mythological friezes and whimsical pastoral scenes, makes this the most enchanting city palace. Don't miss the music library, packed with over 100,000 volumes.

Palazzo della Mercanzia

MUSEO CIVICO D'ARTE INDUSTRIALE E GALLERIA DAVIA BARGELLINI

Beside the Palazzo Sanguinetti looms the **Torre degli Oseletti**, a medieval tower which was originally 70m (230 ft) tall. At the junction of Strada Maggiore and Piazza Aldrovandi, you are unlikely to miss the 'Palace of the Giants', **Palazzo Davia Bargellini**, whose entrance is flanked by two Baroque telamones. The palace is home to the **Museo Civico d'Arte Industriale e Galleria Davia Bargellini** ⓭ (www.museibologna.it/arteantica; Tues–Fri 10am–3pm, Fri 2–6pm, Sat & Sun 10am–6.30pm; free), a collection of applied and decorative arts, and notable Bolognese paintings, many of which belonged to the Bargellini family who started collecting in 1500. Works include Vitale da Bologna's famous *Madonna dei Denti* (*Madonna of the Teeth*), *Pietà* (1368) by his contemporary Simone dei Crocifissi, and the *Giocatori di Dadi* (*The Dice Players*) by Giuseppe Maria Crespi (1740), who specialized in genre scenes with vivid chiaroscuro effects. The last room holds an eighteenth-century Bolognese puppet theatre.

MOZART AND MARTINI

In Room 3 of the Museum of Music, you can find memorabilia of the young Mozart, including two versions of his entrance exam to the Accademia Filarmonica di Bologna. His written test did not comply with the strict academic rules, so Father Giambattista Martini, who had taught Mozart and recognized his genius, secretly handed him the correct version. The museum has two versions of his test below his portrait, one of which includes several mistakes. Mozart came to Bologna twice in 1770 when he was 14. On the first occasion, he performed a private concert for Count Pallavicini in his palace in Via San Felice and stayed at the *Albergo del Pellegrino*, which no longer exists.

Gothic Santa Maria dei Servi

SANTA MARIA DEI SERVI

Across the road is the lovely Gothic **Santa Maria dei Servi** ⓮ (Mon–Fri 7am–12.20pm & 4–6.30pm, Sat & Sun 9–11am & 4–8pm; free), graced by an elegant portico. Work on the church started in 1346 but it was almost two centuries before completion. The most interesting works of art lie behind the elaborate altar, including (on the right side) fragment frescoes on the ceiling by Vitale da Bologna and, in a chapel on the left which you have to light up, an *Enthroned Madonna* (1280–90) traditionally attributed to the great Tuscan master Cimabue, but now thought to be from his workshop.

SANTO STEFANO

From Strada Maggiore, the **Corte Isolani** ⓯, entered beneath the portico of Casa Isolani, is a bijou warren that runs into Via Santo Stefano. Gentrification has turned this cluster of medieval palaces into chic art galleries, desirable apartments, wine bars and cafés. **Via Santo Stefano** is every bit as gracious as Strada Maggiore, with late Gothic palaces once favoured by Bolognese silk merchants. Regular upward glances often reveal twelfth-century tower-houses incorporated in late-medieval residences and embellished with Renaissance facades. **Piazza Santo Stefano** ⓰ is a gentrified neighbourhood square (though more triangular than square), at its most convivial during an antiques market or gourmet food fair. This exclusive enclave numbers the once-radical politician, Romano Prodi, among its ranks – proof, if needed, that politically red Bologna now prefers pale pink.

The cobbled piazza forms the intimate backdrop to **Santo Stefano** ⓱ (Tues–Sun 9.30am–12.30pm & 2.30–7pm, winter until 6pm; free), the city's most hallowed spot. You will need plenty of time to appreciate and work out this ecclesiastical labyrinth, with its feast of ancient and medieval churches. Originally, it was a complex of seven churches in one, as at Jerusalem, and it is known as Le Sette Chiese ('the Seven Churches') despite the fact that only four survive.

The complex dates back at least to the fifth century and may have been founded by Bishop Petronius as his cathedral on the site of a former pagan temple. His corpse was discovered here

Piazza Santo Stefano

in 1141. The Lombards established their religious centre here; it then became a Benedictine sanctuary in the tenth century. Santo Stefano is still run by Benedictines who visibly soften when talking of the basilica's enduring appeal.

A harmonious ensemble is created by the interlocking churches and courtyards, including the Benedictine cloisters, graced by an elegant well head. Seen from the beautiful Piazza Santo Stefano, the larger church on the right is the Chiesa del Crocifisso (Church of the Crucifix), the one in the middle the Church of San Sepolcro modelled on Jerusalem's Holy Sepulchre, and on the left Santi Vitale e Agricola, the oldest church in Bologna. Enter through the **Chiesa del Crocifisso**, of Lombard origin but which has undergone the biggest transformation. The church ends with a central stairway that climbs to the Presbytery. Steps lead down to a graceful little crypt, built to house the relics of the early Bolognese martyrs Vitale and Agricola who died around 304 AD. Their remains are contained in a golden urn on the altar. A door on the left of the main church leads into the most famous of the churches: the **Basilica of San Sepolcro**, a small and unusual polygonal, surrounded by columns, some of which survive from an ancient pagan temple. The body of St Petronius was found in this church in the mid-twelfth century; his relics used to lie in an urn in the centre of the small chapel but were transferred in 2000 to join the saint's head in the Basilica of San Petronio.

Bathed in mystical light, the eleventh-century **Santi Vitale e Agricola** is most compelling. Unadorned and built of bare brick, it retains the most Romanesque Lombard character of all the churches in the city. It is dedicated to the first Bolognese martyrs, Vitale and Agricola, whose graves were discovered in 393 by the great bishop of Milan, St Ambrose. Adjoining it is the **Cortile di Pilato** (Pilate's Courtyard), a fine brick-walled courtyard with a large marble basin erroneously believed to have been used by Pontius

Pilate to wash his hands. Beneath the arcades are chapels and tombstones. Beyond the courtyard lies the mystery **Martyrium**, a transverse church also named the Holy Cross or Trinity Church. Little is known of its origin and history. As you walk along there are niches that light up, one with a sculpted scene of the *Adoration of the Magi* by the Bolognese artist Simone dei Crocifissi. The courtyard leads into the peaceful Benedictine **cloister**, with two tiers of loggias. In the corner is a tiny museum of early Bolognese paintings and reliquaries, and a shop selling liqueurs and lotions made by Carmelite monks.

THE UNIVERSITY QUARTER

The University of Bologna, founded in the eleventh century and famous in its early days for reviving the study of Roman law, is the oldest university in Europe. Petrarch attended classes here, as did Erasmus, Copernicus, various popes and cardinals – and, more recently, Guglielmo Marconi, Enzo Ferrari and Giorgio Armani. It is ranked the number one university in Italy and, today, attracts over 85,000 students annually from around the world. The heart of the student area is the triangle between Via Zamboni and Via San Vitale, but the university quarter also spills out onto Via delle Belli Arti. It is one of the most diverse districts, studded with churches, palaces and museums as well as arty bookshops, eclectic cafés, shabby-chic student dives and graffiti-splashed porticos. The curious Palazzo Poggi, sumptuous seat of the University, is home to imposing temples of scholarship, and the Pinacoteca Nazionale boasts the richest art collection in the region.

A leisurely stroll down Via Zamboni reveals the faculties of modern languages, philosophy, law, economics and the sciences, with each noble palace telling its own story. On the left, at No. 20, is the senatorial sixteenth-century **Palazzo Magnani** ⑱; its hall of honour is adorned with a stunning cycle of frescoes depicting the *The Story of the Foundation of Rome* (1592) by the three Carracci painters, Annibale, Agostino and Ludovico. The two brothers and their cousin worked collaboratively in their early careers, and it is not easy to work out their individual contributions. The palace is the seat of UniCredit Bank but the frieze can be seen on request, at no charge – telephone one day in advance on 051-296 2508.

SAN GIACOMO MAGGIORE

Across the road lies **Piazza Rossini**, named after the composer who studied for three years (1806–9) at the Conservatorio G.B. Martini on the piazza. His first compositions and public performances date from this time, including a historic concert with the opera singer Isabella Colbran, whom he married in 1822.

An ornately decorated portico at the University of Bologna

Gazing out across the square is the church of **San Giacomo Maggiore** ❶ (Mon–Fri 7.30am–12.30pm & 3.30–6.30pm, Sat 9.30am–12.30pm & 3.30–6.30pm, Sun 8.30am–12.30pm & 3.30–6.30pm; free), known as the Bentivoglio family's church. The Romanesque facade and portals, flanked by lions, pre-date Bologna's grandest dynasty, but the elegant Renaissance portico is rooted in their era, as are many of the superb paintings in their family chapel (follow the sign as you enter the church). Although only open on Saturday morning (9.30am–12.30pm), the chapel can be seen through the railings and illuminated by inserting a 50 cent coin. The *Madonna and Child* (1488) and the eerie *Triumph of Death* and *Triumph of Fame* are the work of Ferrarese painter Lorenzo Costa, who worked in Bologna before succeeding Mantegna as the principal painter at the Gonzaga court at Mantua. The *Madonna and Child* (the Bentivoglio Altarpiece) features Giovanni II Bentivoglio, his wife and eleven children, and was allegedly commissioned in thanksgiving for the family's escape from an attempted massacre by a rival family. The *Madonna and Saints* (1494) by Francesco Raibolini, better known as 'Il Francia', is generally regarded as the best of the artist's many altarpieces.

ORATORIO DI SANTA CECILIA

Lorenzo Costa, Il Francia and contemporaries also worked on the **Oratorio di Santa Cecilia** ❷ (Mon–Fri 2–6pm, Sat & Sun 10am–1pm & 2–6pm; free but donations welcome), which adjoins San Giacomo Maggiore and is accessed via the portico. This little gem was built in 1267 but remodelled by the Bentivoglios, who commissioned the artists to portray the *Life and Martyrdom of St Cecilia*, patron saint of music. The lively but little-known Renaissance fresco cycle starts with Cecilia's wedding (far left) and ends with her burial (far right). The scenes are accompanied by the bold statement 'the night after her marriage to a pagan youth, Cecilia revealed that she had taken a vow of chastity and persuaded her husband to convert as she was a bride of Christ'. Even so, the bride met a brutal end, boiled alive, then beheaded as portrayed in the gory decapitation scene on the left as you enter. St Cecilia is patron saint of music so it is appropriate that classical concerts (free of charge) are held in the oratory.

PIAZZA VERDI AND TEATRO COMUNALE

Further along Via Zamboni, **Piazza Verdi** ㉑ is a hub of student life. *Café Scuderia*, with tables spilling out onto the square, is all about chilling out over cheap coffee or beer; the venue often hosts cultural events too. Music often wafts from the **Teatro Comunale** ㉒ (www.tcbo.it), the opera house overlooking the square. Originally called the Nuovo Teatro Pubblico, the theatre was built to replace the wooden Teatro Malvezzi destroyed by fire in 1745. In Renaissance times, this was the site of the sumptuous, 244-room Palazzo Bentivoglio, which was sacked and destroyed in 1507 by the masses who had become discontented with the rule of the Bentivoglio dynasty. The adjoining Via Guasto (*guasto* meaning 'breakdown' or formerly 'devastation') and the modern Giardini del Guasto derived their names from the ruins that laid here for decades. The 1930s facade

Teatro Comunale

Museum of Human Anatomy exhibits

of the Teatro Comunale belies an elegant Baroque-style interior with tiers of boxes (no access apart from performances). Many of these were formerly owned by titled families, each one individually decorated and bearing the family's coat of arms on the ceiling. The opera house played host to twenty operas by Rossini, who lived for many years in Bologna, as well as historic performances such as the premiere of Gluck's *Il Tronfio di Clelia* and the Italian premiere of Verdi's *Don Carlo* in 1867. It was also receptive to works of composers outside Italy, and was the first Italian opera house to stage a Wagner opera, *Lohengrin*, in 1871. Today, it is the city's main venue not only for opera (November to April) but also classical concerts and ballet.

PALAZZO POGGI

In 1803, the university moved from the Archiginnasio (see page 38) to the sixteenth-century **Palazzo Poggi** ❷❸ (Via Zamboni 33; Tues–Fri 10am–4pm, Sat & Sun 10am–6pm; charge only for guided visits of the Specola, the Observatory, for which online reservations are required at www.museospecola.difa.unibo.it). This opulent seat of the university, decorated with Mannerist and early Baroque frescoes, is home to a confusing yet fascinating cluster of museums. In the seventeenth and eighteenth centuries, this was the leading scientific institute in Europe, based on Bologna's history of scholarship, particularly in anatomy and astronomy. A visit to the **Specola** tower on a guided tour (in Italian and English) is highly recommended; it also includes the Specola Museum and its rich collection of instruments for astronomical studies, such as medieval astrolabes and celestial and terrestrial globes. The tower was built on top of the building and served as an astronomical observatory.

The collections served primarily for research rather than as attractions for visitors, but it's worth wandering through the vaulted painted galleries, with cycles of sixteenth-century frescoes, and picking out a few curiosities. Exhibits (many of which now have labels and explanations in English) range from models of military architecture and reconstructions of seventeenth-century warships to precious manuscripts and Japanese woodcuts. But the

MARCONI: BOLOGNA'S WIRELESS PIONEER

Among Bologna University's famous alumni is Guglielmo Marconi (1874–1937), known for his pioneering work on long-distance wireless communication. He was born in Bologna in 1874 to a wealthy Italian landowner and his Irish-Scots wife, but when Italy showed no interest in his experiments or requests for funding, he moved to the UK. At the age of 27, he succeeded in receiving the first transatlantic radio signal, which led to a worldwide revolution in telecommunications. In 1909, Marconi shared the Nobel Prize in Physics for his work on wireless telegraphy. His Marconi Company radios saved hundreds of lives, including the 700 surviving passengers of the sinking *Titanic* in 1912. Bologna's airport was named after him in 1978. Some of Marconi's earliest experiments were completed at the family home, Villa Griffone at Pontechhio Marconi, 15km (9 miles) from Bologna, now home to the Marconi Museum (www. museomarconi.it; guided tours, reservation only).

invariable magnets are the Museums of Obstetrics and Human Anatomy. Set up for teaching surgeons, doctors and midwives in the eighteen century, the collection includes a birthing chair on which blindfolded students would practice medical procedures, as well as terracotta and wax models of wrongly presented foetuses and gruesome models of human dissections.

There is more to see on Via Irnerio to the north of Palazzo Poggi: the university's Botanical Garden, Museum of Physics and the **Luigi Cattaneo Museo delle Cere Anatomiche** (Museum of Anatomic Wax Models; June & July Tues–Fri 10am–1pm; Sept–May Tues–Fri 9am–1pm; free) at No 48, with more waxwork teaching aids, including models of faces with small pox and tumours, human intestines and conjoined twins.

PINACOTECA NAZIONALE

Just north of Palazzo Poggi, on Via delle Belle Arti, is the **Pinacoteca Nazionale** ㉔ (National Art Gallery; www.pinacotecabologna.beni-culturali.it; Sept–June Tues–Sun 9am–7.30pm, July–Aug Tues–Wed 8.30am–2pm, Thurs–Sun 1.45–7.30pm), the finest treasure house in the city. The National Gallery's only flaw is its tendency to close sections for 'lack of personnel'. Created during the Napoleonic occupation, the museum displays paintings plucked from demolished or deconsecrated churches. As was his wont, Napoleon stole many of the finest works for the Louvre but Bologna managed to get them back in 1815. The gallery follows the path of Bolognese and Emilian art from the Middle Ages to the eighteenth century, but also includes pieces by artists from Florence, Tuscany and other 'foreign' parts, showing the influence on local artists.

The itinerary begins with works by Bolognese artists of the four-teenth century, and notably the vigorous and brilliantly coloured *St George and the Dragon* (c.1335) by Vitale da Bologna. Though cast in Byzantine-influenced Gothic mould, this dramatic, stylized

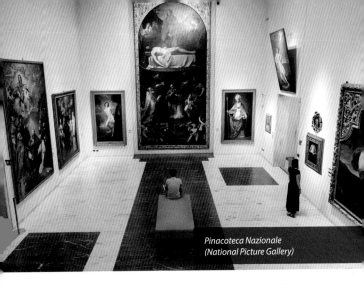

Pinacoteca Nazionale (National Picture Gallery)

scene shows the realism and expressiveness typical of Trecento Bolognese art. Other gallery scene-stealers are Giotto's luminous polyptych, *Madonna and Child with Saints*, which takes pride of place in Room 3 as one of only three panel paintings in the world signed by the artist, and Raphael's *Santa Cecilia* (c.1515) in Room 15. This late altarpiece depicts the early Christian martyr and patron saint of music in ecstasy as she listens to a choir of angels in company of saints and Mary Magdalene. It was commissioned for a chapel dedicated to the saint in Bologna's Augustinian Church of San Giovanni in Monte; from the same church came Parmigianino's *Madonna and Child with Saints* (c.1530), now opposite the Raphael.

Not to be missed are the works by the great Bolognese Baroque artists. Room 23 displays masterpieces by all three of the Carracci painters. The two brothers and their cousin worked collaboratively and their frescoes still adorn the greatest city palaces; but here the works by the individual artists highlight their differences in

Wise words

"When Bologna stops teaching, Bologna will be no more". The words of the Archdeacon of Bologna's cathedral and head chancellor of the Studium (University) in 1687.

style as well as their similarities. Room 24 is dedicated to Guido Reni (1575–1642), including a portrait of his mother and the dramatic and skilful *Massacre of the Innocents*, distinguished by a bold use of colour and grace of line and form.

NORTH AND WEST OF CENTRE

From the maze of streets in the former Jewish ghetto to a cluster of medieval palaces and museums, this area of northern Bologna is packed with cultural attractions. When you have had your fill of sightseeing, the main streets of Via dell'Independenza, Via Ugo Bassi and Via Rizzoli provide plenty of retail distraction.

THE JEWISH GHETTO

Tucked into the triangle of Via Oberdan, Via Zamboni and Via Valdonica, in the shadow of the Due Torri, the former **ghetto** ㉕ is about mood rather than monuments. As a liberal, cosmopolitan city, Bologna welcomed Jews who were booksellers and drapers, but in 1555, under papal rule, the ghetto was established. Unlike the crisply geometric street plan in 'Roman' Bologna, this area is a tangle of narrow alleys, predating the papal edict. Take Via de Giudei (Street of the Jews) to moody Via Canonica and **Via dell'Inferno** ㉖. The appropriately named 'Hell Street' became a virtual prison as only doctors were allowed to leave the ghetto at night. A plaque records the Holocaust but makes no reference to the expulsion of the Jews from here in 1593. The lofty buildings in Via Valdonica reflect the fact that the ghetto could only expand upwards. Recent gentrification has turned these tall tenements into desirable designer pads, so Hell Street is now a prestigious address – and one with a growing number of artisan workshops such as *Calzoleria Max & Gio* at No 22A, creators of fine, made-to-measure shoes for men. The Palazzo Pannolini at 1/5 Via Valdonica is home to the **Museo Ebraico** (Jewish Museum; www.museoebraicobo.it; Sun–Thurs 10am–6pm, Fri 10am–4pm), which aims

BOLOGNA AND THE BAROQUE

The members of the Bolognese school exerted one of the main influences on Baroque painting in Italy in the seventeenth century. Agostino (1557–1602), Annibale (1560–1609) and Ludovico Carracci (1555–1619), two brothers and a cousin, were leading figures in the movement against the affectations of Mannerism in Italian painting. Much in keeping with the desires of the Counter-Reformation, they revived the tradition of solidity and grandeur of the High Renaissance, stressing rigorous draftsmanship from life. Annibale's fame was such that he was called to Rome to decorate the Farnese gallery, considered in its time as a worthy successor to the frescoes of Michelangelo and Raphael. Guido Reni (1775–1642) was a pupil of the Carracci and was initially influenced by their classicizing style. He left Bologna for Rome where he painted many of his finest works, but returned to his native city in 1613 to head a vast studio that exported religious works all over Europe.

In the nineteenth century, the Bolognese painters fell from favour. The leading art critic, John Ruskin, described the school as having "no single virtue, no colour, no drawing, no character, no history, no thought". Their status suffered from Ruskin's attacks but the Carraccis and Guido Reni are now regarded among the greatest Italian painters of their age.

to preserve, study and promote the cultural Jewish heritage of Bologna and the Emilia Romagna region. The history of the Jewish population is analyzed through multimedia exhibits, documents and artefacts from former ghettos.

North of the ghetto, on Piazza San Martino, is **San Martino** (Mon–Sat 8am–noon and 4–7pm, Sun 8.30am–1pm and 4–7pm; free), a Carmelite church remodelled in the fourteenth century along Gothic lines. A quick visit reveals fragments of a Uccello battle scene and paintings by notable Bolognese artists, such as the Carracci. As you trample the cobblestones, look up to spot sealed arches and other vestiges of medieval churches, deconsecrated in Napoleon's day. The square nudges up to **Via Goito**, a popular place with students and a reminder that, for its size, Bologna has the greatest concentration of students in Italy.

An alleyway in the ghetto

CATTEDRALE METROPOLITANA DI SAN PIETRO

Via dell'Indipendenza was built to link the city centre and railway station in 1888. At its southern end the main landmark is the **Cattedrale Metropolitana di San Pietro** ㉗ (Mon–Sat 7am–7pm; Sun 8am–7pm; free). Despite its nominal cathedral status and monumental interior, San Pietro plays second fiddle to the basilica of the city's patron saint, San Petronio. Architecturally and artistically, it is certainly no match. In 1582, Pope Gregory XIII promoted the Bishop of Bologna to Archbishop, and hence the cathedral rose to the rank of 'metropolitan church'. It was remodelled to be a showpiece of papal power and, apart from a few relics in the crypt and the red marble lions from the original portal, there is little trace of the original Romanesque-Gothic structure. Stroll down Via Altabella to see the soaring **bell-tower** which accommodates *'la nonna'* (grandmother), the largest bell playable *'alla bolognese'*, a form of full circle ringing devised in the sixteenth century but which is sadly disappearing.

PALAZZO FAVA

Along **Via Manzoni**, west of Via dell'Indipendenza, the Fava palazzi are among the finest in the city. At No 2, the Palazzo Fava-Ghisilieri is now known simply as **Palazzo Fava** ㉘ (www.genusbononiae. it; Tues–Sun 10am–7pm; access may be limited when exhibitions are not showing; combined ticket available for Palazzo Pepoli, Museo della Storia di Bologna and San Colombano and Tagliavini Collection). The palace was fully renovated as part of the Genus Bononiae project (see page 69), and reopened in 2011 as an exhibition centre. Blockbuster art shows are hosted here, but it is also a treasure house of Carracci frescoes. In 1584, Filippo Fava commissioned Agostino, Annibale and Ludovico Carracci to decorate rooms on the *piano nobile*, which gave rise to the first major fresco cycle of their career. This portrays the tragic tale of *Jason*

Cattedrale Metropolitana di San Pietro

and Medea and adorns the grand Sala di Giasone. Other halls of the palace were later painted with scenes from Virgil's *Aeneid* by Ludovico and his pupils. On the ground floor of the palace, two rooms display changing exhibits from the art collection of the Fondazione Cassa di Risparmio di Bologna.

MUSEO CIVICO MEDIEVALE

Next along is **Palazzo Ghisilardi Fava**, an archetypal Bolognese Gothic palace now home to the **Museo Civico Medievale** ㉙ (Via Manzoni 4; www.museibologna.it/arteantica; Tues & Thurs 10am–2pm, Wed & Fri 2–7pm, Sat & Sun 10am–7pm), a non-fusty medieval museum whose superbly arrayed medieval and Renaissance treasures illuminate the cultural and intellectual life of the city. A graceful, galleried courtyard leads to a series of elaborately sculpted sarcophagi depicting the greatest medieval scholars, and notably the lecturers in law. The collection's highlights are the coffered ceilings, stone statuary, gilded wood sculptures, and the monumental crosses that once adorned major city crossroads. Among many remarkable works are the *Pietra della Pace* by Corrado Fogolini (1322) in Room 9, celebrating peace between the university and municipality following a period of conflict; the red marble tombstone of Bartolomeo da Vernazza (1348) in Room 11; and the statue of a *Madonna and Child* in polychrome terracotta by Jacopo della Quercia (1410) in Room 12.

More specialist are the bronzes, weaponry, miniatures, medals and musical instruments. The vast and bizarre bronze statue of Pope Boniface VIII (1301) by Manno da Siena in Room 7 is a reminder of how the papacy liked to exert its power. Beyond the museum, at No 6, is the Casa Fava Conoscenti, one of the rare surviving tower houses, dating back to the thirteenth century.

SAN COLOMBANO

Just to the west, in Via Parigi, the deconsecrated church complex of **San Colombano** ❸ (www.genusbononiae.it; Wed–Sun 11am–6pm; combined ticket available for Palazzo Pepoli, Museo della Storia di Bologna and Palazzo Fava) makes a beautiful setting for the **Tagliavini Collection** of some eighty historical musical instruments. The late medieval church, awash with faded frescoes, is now filled with the likes of spinets, harpsichords, clavichords and other keyboard instruments dating back five centuries and amassed by Bolognese musician and scholar, Luigi Ferdinando Tagliavini. Remarkably, the instruments are all kept in perfect working order, played regularly and used for free monthly concerts from October to June. Among them are unique pieces such as an early eighteenth-century folding harpsichord and an earlier harpsichord with beautiful landscape decoration inside and out. The Oratory, on the upper level, displays a cycle of frescoes by the School of Carracci. Restoration works revealed the remains of a medieval crypt (accessible to the public) below the church, with a thirteenth-century mural *Crucifixion* attributed to Giunta Pisano and displayed behind glass.

Until Via dell'Indipendenza supplanted **Via Galliera** in 1888, this was the city's most majestic boulevard, built over a Roman road. The arcaded street is lined with noble palaces dating from the fifteen to the eighteenth century. Here, as elsewhere, many of the terracotta-hued porticoes are built of recycled Roman and medieval

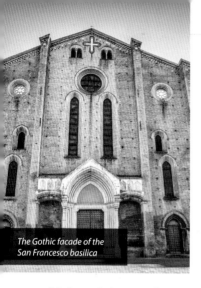

The Gothic facade of the San Francesco basilica

bricks scored with decorative motifs in baked clay. The street runs north to the striking **Porta Galliera** (gateway), repeatedly destroyed and rebuilt five times between 1330 and 1511.

MAMBO

On the northwestern edge of the centre, transformed from a former municipal bakery which supplied bread to the Bolognesi during World War I, is **MAMbo** ③ (Museo d'Arte Moderna di Bologna, Bologna Modern Art Museum; Via Don Minzoni 14; www.mambo-bologna.org; Tues & Wed 2–7pm, Thurs till 8pm, Fri–Sun 10am–7pm). The museum forms part of the cultural **Manifattura delle Arti** complex, transformed from the old harbour and industrial area of the city.

MAMbo hosts temporary exhibitions and has a permanent collection tracing the history of Italian art from World War II to the present day. It is also currently housing the collection of the **Museo Morandi** – transferred from Palazzo d'Accursio in the centre while its galleries are undergoing restoration (no date for completion has been announced). Giorgio Morandi (1890–1964) was one of the great still-life painters of modern times. This collection spans his Cézanne-influenced early works, his moody landscapes and his enigmatic bottles and bowls.

Some of his less-opaque works are landscapes of the Bolognese hills, where the artist withdrew in the face of Fascism. Morandi fans can also now visit the carefully restored house where Morandi lived and worked for most of his life, **Casa Morandi** at 36 Via Fondazza, on the southeastern edge of the city (visits are strictly by appointment only, tel: 051-649 6611 or email casamorandi@comune.bologna.it).

SAN FRANCESCO

Feeling far removed from the city bustle, to the west of the centre, is the Gothic **San Francesco** ㉜ (Mon–Sat 6.45am–noon & 3.30–7pm, Sun 6.45am–1pm & 3.30–7pm; free). Despite radical

A SUBTERRANEAN SERENISSIMA

It might not look like Venice, but Bologna has an intricate network of over 60km (37 miles) of waterways, most of them running underground. From medieval times, water was the source of economic progress and prosperity. The waters of the Savena, Reno and Aposa rivers were harnessed into canals both for domestic use and to provide energy for trades, particularly for the mills of the flourishing textile industry. Bologna became a leading silk producer in the fifteenth century, and at the height of the industry had over one hundred silk mills. The waterways were filled in during the nineteenth century, but a port on the Navile Canal lugged goods and passengers down to the Po River and on to Venice, a system that served the city until the early twentieth century. For a glimpse back into the era of waterways, head for the Via Piella, just south of Piazza VIII Agosto, where the picturesque view over the Reno Canal from the little 'window' on the bridge gives a fleeting impression of Venice. For self-guided, waterway-themed tours visit www.bolognawelcome.com, and for guided tours (in English and Italian) try www.amicidelleacque.org.

Pick up a picnic

The covered Mercato delle Erbe, at Via Ugo Bassi 25, (www.mercatodelleerbe. eu) is a great place for picnic supplies, with its *salumerie* (for *prosciutto* and cheeses), bakers, *enotecas* and colourful stalls piled high with fresh fruit and veg. Alternatively, there's a popular food court for freshly prepared, affordable dishes.

restoration and serious damage during Allied bombings in 1943, the Franciscan church remains one of the most beautiful in the city. Completed in 1263, it is now admired for its rebuilt Gothic facade, ornate altarpiece and Renaissance tombs, including, in the left aisle, the tomb of Pope Alexander V who died in Bologna in 1410. The precious marble altarpiece, depicting saints and naturalistic scenes from the life of St Francis, was the work of the Venetian artists, Pier Paolo and Jacobello dalle Masegne (1393).

Outside, on the street side of the church, are the four raised **Tombs of the Glossatori** (legal annotators), dating from the thirteenth century. Before the university had a fixed abode, students attended lectures in monastic churches, including this one, where medicine and arts were taught. The university's presence lived on in the tombs of these illustrious doctors of law and medicine.

SOUTH OF THE CENTRE

The cultural big-hitter of the city's southern quarter is San Domenico, a convent complex and treasure house of art. The winding Via Castiglione at its northern tip is lined by imposing mansions from various eras, including the fortress-like medieval Palazzo Pepoli, which has been reinvented as a modern history museum. Many of the terracotta-hued palazzi afford glimpses of vaulted courtyards, sculpted gateways and richly frescoed interiors. West of San Domenico, Via Marsili and Via d'Azeglio form part of the city's *passeggiata*, or ritual stroll, a chance to see the city at its most sociable.

The Piazza della Mercanzia, south of the Due Torri, feeds into the noble end of **Via Castiglione**. Both this street and Via Farini, an elegant shopping street, conceal waterways. The canal network, linked to the River Po and the Adriatic, generated the power for the silk and paper mills, brickworks and tanneries, and for the millers, dyers and weavers who were the mainstay of the medieval economy. But when the district was gentrified in the sixteenth century, the nobility scorned these murky waters. Although finally covered in 1660, the canal still runs below Via Castiglione, which explains why the pavements resemble canal banks.

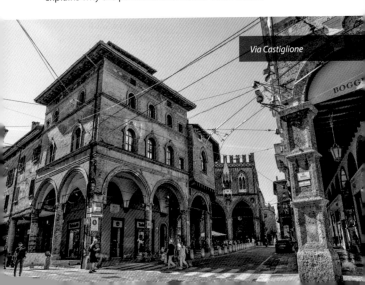

Via Castiglione

The Fiera district

Northeast of centre, the Bologna Exhibition Centre (www.bolognafiere.it) was built in 1961–75 beyond the ring road. It extends over 375,000 sq m (4,036,466 sq ft) and hosts around 30 exhibitions a year. During the most popular shows, hotels in Bologna are booked up months in advance.

The austere medieval facade of the **Palazzo Pepoli Vecchio**, at No 8 Via Castiglione, belies a brand new interior, which is now home to the interesting **Museo della Storia di Bologna** ㉝ (Museum of the History of Bologna; www.genusbononiae.it; Tues–Sun 10am–7pm; combined ticket available for Palazzo Fava, Palazzo delle Esposizioni and San Colombano and Tagliavini Collection see pages 61 and 63). The grandiose palace was built as the seat of the Pepoli, lords of Bologna in the mid-fourteenth century, but was not actually completed until 1723. The fading interior underwent a total transformation in 2012, when the building was reimagined as an innovative, interactive museum, dedicated to the historical and cultural heritage of Bologna.

The fascinating tour spans a whopping 2500 years of the city's distinguished history, and is arranged around the futuristic steel-and-glass Torre del Tempo (Tower of Time), which shoots up from the courtyard. The museum traces the evolution of the city, from the Etruscans to the present day, through an engaging mix of 3D films and cartoons, mock-ups of Etruscan and Roman roads, photos and multimedia installations.

The lively modern displays tend to attract more school groups and students than tourists, and most of the labelling and videos are in Italian (though there are information sheets in English in most rooms).

BASILICA DI SAN DOMENICO

As you walk south along the Via Castiglione, the mood becomes subtly more domesticated. This was the key route to the Bolognese hills, and access here was controlled by Porta Castiglione, one of ten surviving city gates. To the west, the monumental **Basilica di San Domenico** ❸ (Mon–Sat 9am–noon & 3.30–6pm, Sun 3.30–5pm; charge for presbytery only) dominates the cobbled **Piazza San Domenico**. The two mausoleums on the square, each with its tomb raised on pillars and protected by a canopy, celebrate renowned medieval law scholars Rolandino de' Passaggeri and Egidio Foscherari.

The Basilica was built to house the relics of San Domenico, founder of the Dominican order, who died here in 1221 when it was just the small church of San Nicolò of the Vineyards on the outskirts of Bologna. He was canonized in 1234 and his remains lie in

GENUS BONONIAE, MUSEUMS IN THE CITY

The Museo della Storia di Bologna is one of the eight cultural attractions on the 'Genus Bononiae Museums in the City' itinerary (www.genusbononiae.it). The route takes in some of the city's most important churches and palaces that have been completely renovated for public use. Apart from one, all are within easy walking distance in the city centre. The attractions include the Palazzo Fava (see page 61) and the churches of San Colombano with the Tagliavini Collection (see page 63), Santa Maria della Vita (see page 41) and Santa Cristina, where concerts are held. Just out of town is San Michele in Bosco, a former monastery poised on a hill overlooking the city. The churches and palaces on the itinerary are managed (and some also owned) by the Fondazione Cassa di Risparmio di Bologna, a non-profit bank foundation.

an exquisite shrine within the church. The Dominican foundation was built in 1228–38 but was remodelled in Baroque style. Although it has lost much of its late Romanesque and Renaissance purity, it abounds in curious, canopied tombs and artworks by such luminaries as Michelangleo, Pisano and Filippino Lippi as well as by leading Bolognese artists. The **Cappella di San Domenico** (Chapel of St Dominic), holding the saint's tomb, is halfway down the basilica on the right. The spectacular **Arca di San Domenico** (Tomb of St Dominic) is the work of various leading artists, among them Niccolò da Bari – who acquired the name Niccolò dell'Arca following his acclaimed work on this tomb – Nicola Pisano and Arnolfo di Cambio, both of the Pisan School. Niccolò da Bari died in 1492, and the Arca was completed by Michelangelo (a 19-year-old whippersnapper at the time) who carved two Bolognese saints – St Proculus and St Petronius – holding a model of Bologna, and the angel on the right of the altar table holding up the candelabra. Above the Arca, Guido Reni's *St Dominic in Glory with Christ, the Madonna and Saints* decorates the dome, and hidden behind the shrine lies the precious reliquary of the head of St Dominic. Among the other artworks are the *Crucifix* (1250) by Giunta Pisano and the tomb of Taddeo Pepoli, both in the left transept; the *Mystical Marriage of St Catherine* by Filippino Lippi

Basilica di San Domenico

in the small chapel beyond the right transept; and the beautiful mid-sixteenth-century marquetry choir stalls.

VIA D'AZEGLIO

In the early evening, the pedestrianized **Via d'Azeglio** , west of San Domenico, comes alive as locals gather at the bars of the affectionately named *il salotto* (drawing room) for shopping and cocktails. It is a relaxed mix of families and Bologna *per bene* – the smart set. There

Saintly statue on Piazza San Domenico

are big-name boutiques here, but the most exclusive shops are clustered in neighbouring Galleria Cavour and Via Farini. Wedged between the designer stores is the boldest of Bologna's senatorial palaces – the fifteen-century **Palazzo Bevilacqua** (No 31), decked out in Tuscan style with a rusticated sandstone facade, wrought-iron balconies and a courtyard surrounded by a loggia. Here, the Council of Trent met for two sessions in 1547 after fleeing an epidemic in Trent.

Tucked away in a corner west of Via d'Azeglio lies a curious Spanish enclave. The crenellated **Collegio di Spagna** (visits on request) was founded in 1365 by Cardinal Gil de Albornoz (representing the papacy) and bequeathed to Spanish scholars at Bologna University in 1365 as a glorified hostel. It continues to fulfil this function today, under the auspices of the Spanish Crown. Nearby, the peaceful **Caffè de la Paix** welcomes Spanish scholars with open arms. To the north, on the corner of Via Val d'Aposa and Vicolo Spirito

A national icon

If you happen to be in Via d'Azeglio at 6pm, you will hear the music of Lucio Dalla (1943–2012), the much-loved Bolognese singer-songwriter (his *Caruso* sung by Pavarotti sold nine million copies). The music is streamed from Via d'Azeglia 15, where Dalla lived. His funeral was held in the Basilica of San Petronio, and over 50,000 people came to the piazza to bid him farewell.

Santo, the **Spirito Santo** (no admission) is an exquisite jewel-box of a church. Under the medieval streets here runs a secret river, the d'Aposa.

THE BOLOGNA HILLS

Crowning a hilltop to the southwest of the city and linked to it by the world's longest portico is the spectacular **Santuario della Madonna di San Luca** ㊱ (daily 7am–6pm; church: free, terrace: donation). Dating from 1732, the conspicuous pink basilica took fifty years to build, is 3.8km (2.3 miles) long, has a whopping 666 arches and wends its way up from Piazza di Porta Saragozza. You are rewarded at the top with fine views of the Apennines. If you don't fancy the whole hike, take bus #20 to the Arco Meloncello and walk from there, or hop on board the little tourist train from the centre in season. The eighteenth-century sanctuary is richly decorated and houses a much-revered Byzantine-style image of the Madonna, probably dating from medieval times but once believed to have been painted by St Luke. Every Ascension Week, she is carted down the hill to the Cathedral of San Pietro, with crowds lining the Via Saragozza to watch the procession go by. The church brings barefoot pilgrims and other worshippers, as well as joggers and cyclists who battle up the hill to work off the bowls of pasta.

Lording it over Bologna to its south is **San Michele in Bosco** ③ (daily 8am–noon and 4–6pm; free; 30 mins on foot or take No 30 bus), a religious complex with an annexed monastery that has served as an orthopaedic hospital since 1880. The Fondazione Cassa di Risparmio di Bologna now manages the vast area, including the octagonal cloister and library, and the church features on the Genus Bononiae museum itinerary (see page 69). The sweeping views, which were admired by Stendhal when he passed through Bologna in 1817, embrace the entire city.

EXCURSIONS FROM BOLOGNA

Thanks to excellent rail links, Bologna makes a good base for excursions to the handsome historic cities of Emilia-Romagna. It

Santuario della Madonna di San Luca

is only half-hour to Modena and Ferrara, an hour to Parma, 80 mins to Ravenna and 90 mins to Rimini. The region is a gourmet's wonderland, and many visitors sign up for gastronomic tours taking in artisan producers of Parma ham, *Mortadella*, the traditional balsamic vinegar of Modena and Parmigiano Reggiano. The Langhirano valley cradles around 500 authorized producers of the famous *prosciutto crudo di Parma*, many open to the public for tastings. Parmesan cheese-makers pepper the plains north of Parma, while the countryside surrounding Modena is littered with balsamic vinegar distilleries where the vinegar is aged in wooden barrels for up to 25 years.

PARMA

Parma ③⑧ is a byword for fine living, from Parmesan and Parma ham to music and Mannerist art. Unfurling from the historic core of the city, a knot of quiet old streets opens out onto the harmonious **Piazza Duomo**, where the Lombard Romanesque **Cathedral** (www.piazzaduomoparma.com; daily 10am–noon & 3–6pm; church: free, baptistery: charge) and the graceful rose marble Baptistery form a fine ensemble. Inside the cathedral, Correggio's great masterpiece, the magnificent *Assumption of the Virgin* (1526–30), decorates the central dome in a glorious triumph of *trompe-l'œil*.

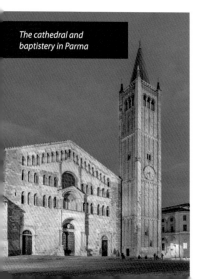
The cathedral and baptistery in Parma

This boldly illusionistic work – Correggio's last fresco – paved the way for Baroque art but found little favour with the church. The neighbouring **Baptistery** (open daily 10am–6pm) is an absolute jewel of the Italian Romanesque style – a beautiful octagonal building etched with elaborately carved reliefs on the exterior and portals by esteemed sculptor and architect, Benedetto Antelami (1150–1230).

Frogs' legs fresco

A canon of Parma's cathedral criticized Correggio's fresco of the *Assumption of the Virgin* as 'a stew of frogs' legs', but Titian, recognizing the artist's triumph of illusionism, decreed that if the dome were turned upside down and filled with gold it would not be as valuable as Correggio's frescoes.

The interior is an illuminated manuscript awash with vividly coloured thirteenth-century biblical scenes, influenced by Byzantine art. Antelami and his assistants created the series of intricate sculptures, showing the seasons, the signs of the zodiac and the labours of the month. The masterly Antelami is also believed to have been the architect of the Baptistery.

In the shadow of the cathedral, the sixteenth-century Renaissance church of **San Giovanni Evangelista** (daily 8.30–11.45am & 3–6pm) has a Baroque facade rising up to meet a cupola decorated with the fine Correggio fresco: *The Vision of St John on Patmos*, depicting Christ descending to John. Northwest of Piazza del Duomo, in a former Benedictine convent, the **Camera di San Paolo** (Mon–Sat 1.10–6.50pm) was one of the private rooms in the apartments of the unconventional and learned Abbess of San Paolo, Giovanna da Piacenza. In 1519, she commissioned Correggio to decorate the room with a feast for the senses, including mischievous *putti* and a view of Chastity as symbolized by the goddess Diana. It was Correggio's first large-scale commission in Parma.

The **Palazzo della Pilotta** on Piazzale della Pace is the city's cultural heart. The beautiful palace is home to the **Galleria Nazionale** (Tues–Sun 10.30am–7pm), hung with works by locals such as Correggio and Il Parmigianino, along with Venetian, Tuscan and other Emilian artists. The palazzo also houses the archeological museum, brimming with pre-Roman and Roman artefacts, the Palatine Library and the **Teatro Farnese**, an imposing wooden theatre with a revolving stage, based on Palladio's masterpiece, the Teatro Olimpico at Vicenza. It is still used for theatrical performances.

MODENA

Modena ㊴ is the home of Pavarotti, Maserati and Ferrari, and its wonderfully preserved historic centre is a Unesco World Heritage Site. Yet it is rarely visited by tourists. The success of the food, purring Ferrari cars and ceramics industries has been instrumental in making tourism a mere afterthought in this cosseted land of plenty. A morning's sightseeing in the historic centre could be followed by a meal at *Osteria Francescana*, the fine-dining restaurant that scooped the much-coveted No 1 spot in the World's 50 Best Restaurants in 2018 (see page 114 and reserve well in advance), then perhaps a visit to the traditional balsamic vinegar distillery, **Acetaia di Giorgio** (Via Cabassi 67; www.acetaiadigiorgio.it) to learn the tricks of the trade and taste the unctuous Aceto Balsamico Tradizionale di Modena.

Modena's city centre is dominated by the majestic **Duomo** (daily 7.30am–12.30pm & 3.30–7pm), one of the masterpieces of the Italian Romanesque for both its architecture and sculpture. The grandiose marble cathedral and adjoining bell tower are Unesco World Heritage Sites. In a tribute, rare for the twelfth century, the names of both the architect, Lanfranco, and the master sculptor, Wiligelmo da Modena, are recorded on inscriptions on the facade.

Countess Matilda of Tuscany, ruler of Modena from 1055–1115, commissioned Lanfranco, the greatest architect of the time, to mastermind the cathedral that would house the remains of St Geminiano, patron saint of the city. Wiligelmo equalled him in creating the exuberant friezes of griffins and dragons, peacocks and trailing vine leaves. On the southern side, the main portal is flanked by stylized Roman-style lions; over the doorway on the left is Wiligelmo's finest work, the depiction of the *Creation and Fall of Adam and Eve*.

To the north, the sculptured Porta della Pescheria is decorated with the cycle of the months. The softly lit interior reveals

Modena's Piazza Grande

Pavarotti's house

The House and Museum of Luciano Pavarotti, 8km (5 miles) from the centre of Modena (www. casamuseolucianopavarotti. it) gives a glimpse into the life of the late maestro. Spend an enjoyable couple of hours perusing the personal memorabilia and listening to recordings of great performances.

brick-vaulted naves and such treasures as the rood-screen, a Romanesque gem, as well as the crypt sculpted by Wiligelmo. Alongside the apse rises the leaning **Torre della Ghirlandina**, the octagonal twelfth-century bell tower built with slabs of marble recycled from Roman ruins. To the northwest of the cathedral, on Piazza Sant'Agostino, stands the **Palazzo dei Musei** (www. museicivici.modena.it), where the d'Este court amassed Modena's finest art collection and library, and now host to the city's museums and art galleries. The most diverting are the **Galleria Estense** (www.gallerie-estensi. beniculturali.it; Tues–Sat 10am–5.30pm, Sun 10am–5.30pm), a rich curation of works by Emilian, Flemish and Venetian artists, and the **Biblioteca Estense** which displays rare manuscripts, seals and maps, as well as the priceless Bibbia di Borso – the beautifully illustrated bible of Borso d'Este, first Duke of Modena.

On Piazza Roma, northeast of the cathedral, the austere and immense **Palazzo Ducale** (Ducal Palace) was the former court of the d'Este dynasty. It is now Italy's top military academy, with no access for the public, but the ducal park behind has been converted into public and botanical gardens.

FERRARI MUSEUMS

Ferrari, Maserati and Lamborghini sports cars are all produced in Modena so a passion for speed goes with the territory. Enzo Ferrari founded his firm in 1939, and the company is still producing cars in the Maranello factories in the industrial outskirts. Modena now has its own Ferrari museum: the **Museo Enzo Ferrari** (https://musei.ferrari.com/en/modena), where Ferraris and Maseratis are displayed in a gigantic showroom, and Enzo Ferrari's fascinating life story is related in the converted workshop of his father. A regular shuttle bus connects the museum with Maranello (20km/12.5 miles from Modena), where the **Museo Ferrari** (https://musei.ferrari.com/en/maranello) showcases the world's largest collection of Ferraris, with models through the ages – and a simulator where visitors can experience driving a Ferrari single-seater on the Monza track. Every Ferrari victory in the Grand Prix is celebrated by the priest ringing the bells of the Maranello parish church – which gives you some idea of the fanaticism of the locals.

FERRARA

Beguiling **Ferrara** ④ was a stronghold of the high-living dukes of Este – archetypically scheming, murderous, Renaissance villains who ruled from 1200–1600 and from Ferrara-controlled territory embracing Parma, Modena and Garfagnana in Tuscany. During its Renaissance heyday, the dynasty drew artists of the stature of Piero della Francesca and Mantegna, turning the Ferrara court into a 'princely

Museum Enzo Ferrari

On your bike

Ferrara is Italy's most bike-friendly city – there are around 2 bikes per inhabitant. For bike hire, cycling suggestions in the traffic-free centre and cycling tourism in the province (including the popular 100km/62.5 mile route that runs along the River Po towards the sea), visit www.ferraraterraeacqua.it.

garden of delights'. From the seventeenth to the nineteenth century, travellers found Ferrara something of a ghost town with few inhabitants and grass growing in the deserted streets. However, since its bombing in World War II, the city underwent a revival and in 1995, it was declared a Unesco World Heritage Site.

The heart of the town is still dominated by the formidable **Castello Estense** (www.castelloestense.it; Wed–Mon 10am–6pm), a fourteenth-century moated fortress where guides regale delightfully dubious tales of what went on in the dungeons. As the d'Este dynasty's seat, the medieval fortress was gradually transformed into a gracious Renaissance palace, but retains elements from both incarnations. Most of the artistic treasures were spirited away to Modena when Ferrara's rival became the Ducal capital in 1598, and the great works of the Ferrarese school are scattered throughout European public collections, notably the National Gallery in London. However, the noble apartments are crowned by some outstanding frescoed ceilings. To sample noble dishes dating back to the d'Este court, head for the unassuming **Hostaria Savonarola** in Piazza Savonarola, nudging up to Castle Square. Try a plate of *tortelli di ricotta* or *cappellacci di zucca,* pumpkin-filled pasta parcels.

South of the Castello Estense is the triple-gabled Romanesque and Gothic **Cathedral** (temporarily closed for renovation; free). The facade is scored with rich sculptural detail, from the lunette of *St George Killing the Dragon* to the loggia and the baldachin adorned with sculptures of the Madonna and Child. Inside does not live up the promise: the Baroque interior is disappointing, though somewhat redeemed by a Byzantine baptismal font and the museum. The latter holds sculptures by Jacopo della Quercia, and two masterpieces by Cosmè Tura decorating organ shutters and representing *The Annunciation* and *St George and the Princess*. The **Piazza della Cattedrale** is best appreciated from the café terrace of the *Pasticceria Leon d'Oro*. The square comes alive during the Palio in May, a medieval tournament dating back to 1259, and, in August, the Buskers' Festival – the biggest of its kind in the world.

Almost every vermillion brick palazzo in Ferrara has a link to the powerful dynasty. You can get a sense of their grandeur among the Renaissance palazzi of the Corso Ercole I d'Este, part of an ambitious fifteenth-century urban expansion, Addizione Erculea. The d'Estes' **Palazzo dei Diamanti** (www.palazzodiamanti.it; Mon–Fri 9am–1pm, Tues & Thurs also 3–5pm) takes its name from the 8500 diamond-shaped marble stones studding its facade. The palace stages prestigious modern-art exhibitions and is also home to the **Pinacoteca Nazionale** (National Picture Gallery; www.

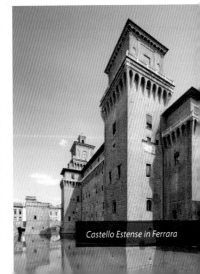

Castello Estense in Ferrara

gallerie-estensi.beniculturali.it; Tues–Sun 10am–5.30pm), which displays frescoes from several ruined churches and School of Ferrara paintings by Cosmè Tura and Francesco del Cossa.

The main thoroughfare, **Corso Giovecca**, has a sweep of patrician palaces designed to connect the medieval core with the Renaissance city. The most regal residence is **Palazzina di Marfisa d'Este** (Tues–Sun 9.30am–1pm & 3–6pm) which was a *delizia*, a Renaissance pleasure palace dedicated to satisfying every whim. The noble apartments are decked out with Renaissance furniture, a portrait gallery and ceilings studded with grotesque motifs. The frescoed loggia, which is used for concerts, is a nod to the sumptuous rural retreat this once was.

Hugging the south-eastern edge of the city, the fourteenth-century **Palazzo Schifanoia** was once the summer residence of Borso d'Este, Duke of Ferrara. The name translates as 'Palace for Banishing Boredom', a reflection of its role as the d'Este court's hedonist hideaway. The austere facade was once as richly frescoed as the interior. A highlight of the palace-museum is the restored **Salone dei Mesi** (Room of the Months) on the first floor, decorated with a delightful cycle of frescoes depicting the four seasons. Here, allegorical tales are interwoven with everyday court scenes.

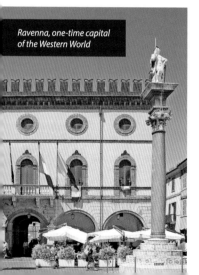

Ravenna, one-time capital of the Western World

RAVENNA

With its air of quiet prosperity, **Ravenna** ⓸ seems like a provincial sleepy town that just happens to contain the finest mosaics in Europe. It is packed with no fewer than an incredible eight Unesco World Heritage Sites in the shape of Byzantine monuments. Like Venice, Ravenna was built on a small archipelago of islands in a lagoon. It thrived as a Roman city, was the last enclave of the Roman Empire in the West and even shone throughout the so-called Dark Ages. In the fifth and sixth centuries, a glorious collision of Roman and Byzantine cultures bequeathed Ravenna superb mosaics, transforming the city into a luminous Western Byzantium. Since the early mosaics were designed by Greek artists from Constantinople, the inspiration was as much from pagan temples as Christian churches.

In the northern corner of the city centre is the three-storey brick **Basilica of San Vitale** (daily: March–Oct 9am–6.45pm; Nov–Feb 9am–4.45pm; ticket includes entry to Basilica of Sant'Apollinare Nuovo, Neoniano Baptistery, Mausoleum of Galla Placidia and Archiepiscopal Museum and Chapel and the opening times are the same). This simple, octagonal-plan brick church, which was consecrated in the sixth century, has an unexpectedly vibrant interior decorated with superb mosaics, remarkable for their clarity of design and colour after all these years and for their extraordinarily intricate detail.

In the same grounds is the oldest of the Byzantine monuments, the fifth-century **Mausoleum of Galla Placidia**, named after the Christian half-sister of Honorius, the Roman emperor who transferred the capital to Ravenna in AD 402. She ruled in the emperor's absence, and later married a Visigoth king and a Roman emperor before returning to Ravenna. This tiny Latin cross-shaped mausoleum has a plain brick exterior that conceals a stunning tapestry of mosaics – the oldest in Ravenna. The mystical atmosphere is intensified by the strikingly simple style of the mosaics, including the cobalt-blue sky sprinkled with gold stars.

East of the city centre, the **Basilica di Sant'Apollinare Nuovo** was built by the Christian Ostrogoth King Theodoric in the sixth century using Greek marbled columns repurposed from a pagan temple. The mosaic-encrusted interior is studded with scenes recalling life in Ravenna and biblical anecdotes. On the left, the paintings depict twenty-two virgins leaving the ancient port of Classe to follow the Three Magi; opposite, the solemn procession of twenty-six martyrs is wonderfully naturalistic, despite a traditional format. Although created in different periods, the mosaics present great unity, infusing Byzantine decorative genius with the awe and mystery of Catholicism. These elements come together in a sublime *Christ in Majesty*.

Approximately 5km (3 miles) south of the city centre stands the grand Byzantine **Basilica di Sant'Apollinare in Classe** (Mon–Sat 8.30am–7.30pm, Sun 1.30–7.30pm). If this sumptuous basilica appears marooned in the countryside, that is because it is symbolic of the abandonment of the site after the silting up of Classe, Rome's largest Adriatic port. The focus of attention is the apse and choir with their breathtaking mosaics, rich with intricate landscape details.

Look out for the docile lambs in the pastoral scene of the Good Shepherd – a reminder that Ravenna was a beacon of artistic excellence at a time when sheep were grazing on the Roman forum. The lustrous tints and textures led Dante, who had sought refuge in Ravenna, to describe the mosaics as having 'the sweet colour of oriental sapphires'.

RIMINI

A long sandy beach, lively hotels and nightclubs make **Rimini** ❷ a breezy summer playground for sun-seeking holiday-makers.

Ponte di Tiberio, Rimini

But head inland to discover a quiet historic centre scattered with Roman and Renaissance monuments. The most prized of them all is the unfinished fifteenth-century **Tempio Malatestiano** (Mon–Fri 8.30am–noon & 3.30–6.30pm, Sat 8.30am–12.30pm & 3.30–7pm, Sun 9am–12.30pm & 3.30–6.30pm; free), a Renaissance design created by the famous Florentine architect and art theorist Leon Battista Alberti, who was inspired by the wealth of Roman architecture remaining in the city. More pagan temple than church, Tempio Malatestiano served as a mausoleum for the cultivated but cruel tyrant Sigismondo Malatesta and his wife Isotta degli Atti.

Now the city cathedral, the Tempio showcases a crucifix attributed to Giotto, as well as Piero della Francesca's fresco of *Sigismondo Malatesta Kneeling before his Patron Saint Sigismondo* (1451) and the sculpted Malatesta tombs – works far finer than the debauched rulers deserved.

Designer stores flank Portico
del Pavaglione

THINGS TO DO

ENTERTAINMENT

Bologna is lively all year-round, but particularly from March to June and September to December when the cultural season is in full swing. The huge student population ensures that the city has a vibrant nightlife scene – during term-time at least; and during the long summer holiday, when the students abandon the city, the powers-that-be stage a season of music and cinema to content its visitors. Bologna hosts great music, both classical and contemporary, and is the only Italian city to have been dubbed a Unesco Creative City of Music (2006). The tourist office website (www.bolognawelcome.com) is a good source of information for upcoming cultural events and the best nightlife venues.

CLASSICAL MUSIC, OPERA AND THEATRE

The **Teatro Comunale** (Largo Respighi 1; www.tcbo.it) is the main venue for the performing arts, from opera and ballet to orchestral and chamber music. Tickets are available from the box office, the Bologna Welcome tourist office in Piazza Maggiore or online. Concerts are also organized in the city's theatres, churches and at the **Conservatorio G.B. Martini** (Piazza Rossini 2; www.consbo. it), a concert hall within a repurposed Augustine convent. Many churches, such as Santo Stefano, San Domenico, Santa Maria dei Servi and Santa Cristina, moonlight as concert venues.

The frescoed **Museo Internazionale e Biblioteca della Musica** (Strada Maggiore 34; www.museibologna.it) is both an exceptional museum of music and a stage for classical concerts and events; likewise the restored church of **San Colombano** is home to the Tagliavini collection of historical musical instruments and hosts

The annual open-air film festival in Piazza Maggiore

free monthly classical recitals from October to June. The central **Auditorium Teatro Manzoni** (Via De'Monari 1/2; www.tcbo.it), set within a finely restored Art Nouveau palazzo, hosts a range of concerts from classical to jazz, rock and contemporary. The **Teatro Europa** (Piazza Costituzione 4; www.teatroeuropa.it), near the Fiera exhibition centre, is the place to go for ballet, musicals and drama.

CINEMA

The **Cineteca di Bologna** (www.cinetecadibologna.it) can be found within the reimagined Manifattura Tabacchi, a former tobacco factory on the northwest edge of the city that's been converted into a major cultural centre. The Cineteca's state-of-the-art Cinéma Lumière (with the Sala Scorsese and Sala Mastroianni) honours the history of the moving image, screening restored classics, retrospectives and rare films, always in the original version. The forward-thinking space is always the venue for Bologna's annual film festivals.

Within the same complex is the Renzo Renzi Library, dedicated to the conservation and study of film and photography and the archives of Charlie Chaplin and Pier Paolo Pasolini (viewing by appointment only). The **Capitol** cinema (www.capitolmultisala. com) near the station shows blockbusters in their original version, with Italian subtitles.

NIGHTLIFE

As a lively university city, Bologna has no shortage of bars, pubs, clubs, live jazz venues and late-opening restaurants. The early evening is all about the ritual *passeggiata*, the people-watching parade, partly viewed from a succession of café terraces. In summer, Bologna's parks are transformed into party venues, with the atmosphere resembling a less boisterous version of a German *biergarten*. The most popular spot is **La Montagnola Park**, which puts on live jazz and rock music performances, as well as stalls selling beer, wine and fast food. Open-air concerts, films and festivities are also staged in city squares, such as Piazza Maggiore; other events take place in streets, museums and beneath the porticoes.

In general, the buzziest area in town is the **Via Zamboni** in the student district, which is peppered with after-hours music haunts. The **Via del Pratello** area on the west side of the city also lures late-night revellers to its cluster of pubs and bars (frequently serving food as well as drinks), interspersed with music clubs and inns. The scene is predominantly student-orientated, though a

APERITIVO TIME

Cocktails are part of Bolognese nightlife and Happy Hour is a moveable feast, from 6–9.30pm. The price of a drink may seem steep, but *stuzzichini* (appetizers) and often a whole buffet may be included, and can provide a meal in itself. A favourite tipple is an Aperol spritz, made with orange liqueur, prosecco and a splash of soda. Among the most popular cocktail spots are: *Zanarini* behind the Basilica, rendezvous of well-heeled Bolognesi, and *Eataly*, the popular 'marketplace' Italian chain at Via degli Orefici. But the most unusual spot has to be the atmospheric *Le Stanze* (see page 112), housed within a Bentivoglio chapel.

clutch of bar-restaurants appeals to all ages. A standout example is **Cantina Bentivoglio** (www.cantinabentivoglio.it), where the best jazz in Bologna reverberates in palatial sixteenth-century cellars. Jazz has thrived in the city since the arrival of American troops at the end of World War II, and can be heard in many other *osterie* throughout the city.

SHOPPING

Bologna's best buys are food and wine, fashion and designer goods. Shopping here is anything but provincial, and ranges

PASTA PERFECT

What better souvenir of your trip to Italy's foodie capital than to be able to recreate perfect handmade pasta back home? Bologna has over twenty cookery schools, which is perhaps not surprising in what is generally regarded as the culinary capital of Italy. A half-day course might take in a tour of the local market, with its fresh produce and gourmet delis (including tastings on the way), and a lesson on how to make an authentic *ragù alla bolognese* (bolognese sauce) and prepare the egg pasta from scratch. After all the hard work, you can sit back and enjoy the fruits of your labour – along with a glass or two of good *vino*. The hands-on sessions are adapted to level of experience and culinary requirements; they are usually held in small groups and last a couple of hours, a half or whole day or longer. A few days' notice may be required, though last-minute requests are always worth trying. Costs vary considerably from €90–160 for a half-day class (followed by lunch, which is included in the price). Full details are available from the Bologna Welcome tourist office (www.bolognawelcome.com).

from one-off independents to top designer brands – many of which started out in the city or in the wider region. Bologna's upmarket clothes outlets are all central, and clustered around the Piazza Maggiore area, some in beautifully restored palazzi. The pedestrianized Via d'Azeglio is a lovely place to shop, as is Via dell'Archiginnasio, the porticoed area behind San Petronio known as the Pavaglione. The smartest

Style icon Giorgio Armani was born in Piacenza

boutiques line Via Farini and the discreet shopping galleries nearby. Galleria Cavour, a luxurious arcade linking Via Farini with Via de'Foscherari, is the place to go for the big names. More mainstream shopping, from fashion to footwear, can be found along Via dell'Indipendenza, Via Rizzoli and Via Ugo Bassi, the high streets of Bologna. *Coin*, at Via Rizzoli 7, part of the chain department store, is worth checking out for affordable clothes made in Italy.

GASTRONOMY

Bologna has a dazzling array of gastronomic delicacies. Moreover, Emilia Romagna, as a region, is dedicated to preserving its unique branded produce, from Parmesan cheese and Parma ham to balsamic vinegar, extra-virgin olive oil and wine. All of these can be picked up in delicatessens, markets, or sampled directly from local producers. The Bolognesi attach great importance to finding the right foodstuffs and you are likely to find good quality just about everywhere, even in the simplest street market.

The Bologna Welcome office (www.bolognawelcome.com) has information on gastronomic tours where you can track down tasty cheeses, cured meats, truffles, dried mushrooms and genuine balsamic vinegar – just to name a few. In central Bologna, just off Piazza Maggiore, the warren of alleys making up the **Mercato di Mezzo** is a feast for the eyes with its specialized food shops, stalls piled high with fresh fruit, fish and cheese, and a covered market selling the finest regional produce. Along Via Pescherie Vecchie, Via degli Orefici and Via Drapperie, shopkeepers tempt passers-by with slices of *Mortadella* and *prosciutto*. **Tamburini** (Via Caprarie 1; www.tamburini.com) is the city's most endearing delicatessen, brimming with Bolognese and Emilian specialities. Try its goodies at the VeloCibò self-service. For home-made pasta and bread, look no further than **Paolo Atti & Figli** (Via Caprarie 7; www.paoloatti.com), a Bolognese institution dating back to 1900 and still in the same family. Pastas are all made on the spot, and its beautifully wrapped and boxed creations make perfect Italian gifts to take back home. Also in the heart of the market is **Salumeria Simoni** (Via Drapperie 5/2a; www.salumeriasimoni. it), stacked to the brim with hams and cheeses. A step inside the shop may well tempt you to sign up for one of its gastronomy tours or at least to try out the delicacies with local wine.

Chocoholics should head for **Majani** (Via Carbonesi 5; www. majani.it), one of Italy's oldest chocolate shops whose delicacies were one-time favourites with European royalty. Displays are laid out in a splendid Art-Nouveau shopfront and Art-Deco interior. Try the Fiat Majani, created for the launch of the new Fiat Tipo 4, hence the four decadent layers of velvety chocolate. Another irresistible *chocolatier* is **Roccati** (Via Clavature 17a; www.roccaticioccolato. com), where you can local artisans sculpt the chocolate creations before you in the workshop. Don't miss the signature *gianduja*, chocolate with hazelnut. For divine patisserie, head for **Regina di Quadri** on Via Castiglione (www.pasticceriareginadiquadri.it), with its showstopping cakes and pastries.

Food shopping is serious business in Bologna

Modena is renowned for *aceto balsamico* (balsamic vinegar) but the factory-produced variety made of wine vinegar bears scant resemblance to the traditional product – a subtle, unctuous substance that can only be sold after ageing in wooden casks for at least twelve years (red label), eighteen years (silver label) or twenty-five years (gold label). Look for Aceto Balsamico Tradizionale di Modena or di Reggio Emilia. The real deal is a reduction of pressed and cooked Trebbiano and Lambrusco grapes, characterized by a complex sweet and sour flavour, a hint of wood, and a high price tag. Expect to pay €40–80 for a small bottle, but whether you are using it on Parmigiano Reggiano and *Mortadella* or drizzling it over strawberries or *gelato*, all you'll need is a few drops. Bottles can be bought from *acetaie* (balsamic vinegar producers) in the region or from high-end food shops in Bologna.

A smattering of excellent *enoteche* (specialized wine stores) can be found in the city centre, where you can try and buy local bottles. Try **Enoteca Italiana** (Via Marsala 2b) for its carefully curated selection of Italian and particularly Emilia Romagna wines. It is run by two award-winning sommeliers, who will guide you round and suggest wine pairings for regional treats such as Parma ham and *Mortadella*, which are served here all day.

MARKETS

The city markets are full of character, atmosphere and delicious foodstuffs, ideal for picnics or as presents to take home. In the centre are the **Mercato di Mezzo** and adjoining open-air food market as well as the renovated **Mercato delle Erbe** at Via Ugo Bassi 25, a large and lively covered market with wonderful local produce and a food court where you can sit and feast on a smorgasbord of freshly prepared eats. The **Mercato Antiquario**, spread across Piazza Santo Stefano and the streets nearby, is an antiques and curios market, with vintage clothing and jewellery, held on the second Saturday and Sunday of the month from 8.30am–6pm (7pm in summer, closed July and August). Another antiquarian fixture is the **Mercato dell'Antiquariato** on Via Matteotti, held on the first Tuesday of the month (except for July and August) and, from March to June and September to December, also the third Tuesday of the month. The **DecoMela Art** and **San Giuseppe Colours** on Via San Giuseppe, which take place on alternative weekends (Friday–Sunday, except January, July and Aug), are favoured haunts of handicraft-collectors, with pottery, lamps, fabrics and semi-precious stones. **La Piazzola** market takes over the Piazza VIII Agosto every Friday and Saturday and is worth checking out for bargain shoes and clothes, including vintage one-offs; it also sells leather, bric-à-brac, arts and crafts.

SPORT

Basketball (*pallacanestro*) in Bologna is hugely popular and the city's Virtus team (www.virtus.it) is one of the best in Europe. Tickets are available from www.ticketone.it or at the Unipol Arena

Markets and food stalls abound with locally grown fruit and vegetables

in Casalecchio di Reno, southwest of the city. Their Italian rivals are Fortitudo (in the Second Division), who play at PalaDozza (or 'the Palazzo'), a multipurpose arena with a capacity of 5570 in Piazza Azzarita, northwest of the centre. As elsewhere in Italy, **football** (soccer) is a passion. Bologna FC (Football Club, www.bolognafc.it), in the First Division, has scooped the Italian league championship title seven times, and when they play at home thousands of fans make a beeline for the Renato dall'Ara stadium, Via Andrea Costa 174, about 3km (2 miles) west of the city centre. Tickets can be bought at various tobacconists or online at www.sport.ticketone.it.

MOTOR VALLEY

In the heart of Emilia's 'Land of Motors', with its Ferrari and Lamborghini-inspired museums, Bologna is a petrolhead's dream. The museums can be visited independently by public transport or on a guided tour – details of which can be found at the Bologna

Welcome tourist office (www.bolognawelcome.com). For the Ferrari Museums in Maranello and Modena, see page 78. The **Museo Ferruccio Lamborghini** (www.museolamborghini.com) moved in 2013 from Dosso near Ferrara to Argelato, 15km (9 miles) north of Bologna. Visitors who book ahead can tour the company factory with Fabio Lamborghini, a nephew of the famous founder Ferruccio. For motorbike fans, the **Ducati Museum** at the Ducati Factory (www.ducati.com/it/it/borgo-panigale-experience), 9km (5.5 miles) northwest of the city centre, displays the models that have thrust the brand onto the global stage.

ACTIVE PURSUITS

Few of the central hotels have fitness centres, but there are plenty of outdoor activities to divert you. You could climb the Asinelli

Museo Ferruccio Lamborghini

Tower (498 steps), stretch your legs in the Parco della Montagnola or Giardini Margherita, or walk 6km (4 miles) up to the hilltop sanctuary of San Luca.

The city is well equipped with public swimming pools, including the **Piscina Sterlino** (Via A. Murri 113) southeast of the city, with one Olympic-sized pool, two 25m ones and a green area with bar, parasols and sunbeds in summer. Elsewhere, the **Carmen Longo-Stadio** at Bologna's football stadium centre (Via dello Sport; www.sogese.com) has a complex of indoor and outdoor pools. The **Circolo Tennis Bologna** (Viale Rino Cristiani 2; www.circolotennisbologna.com) in the Margherita Gardens has seven courts, floodlit from April to September and covered for the rest of the year. It also has a 25m swimming pool and a gym. For relaxation and wellbeing, the **Mare Terme San Petronio** (Via Irnerio 12/A; www.maretermalebolognese.it), near Parco della Montagnola, offers thermal spa waters, a sauna, pool, hot tubs and beauty treatments. For those who prefer a Turkish bath, the **Hammam Bleu** (Vicolo Barbazzi 4; www.hammam.it; temporarily closed at the time of writing), centrally located just south of the Basilica of San Petronio, has treatments ranging from basic (€55) to the full works (€185). Booking is essential, as is a membership fee of €10 per person.

SPORTS IN EMILIA ROMAGNA

Emilia Romagna holds its own against even the sportiest of regions, with activities ranging from sailing to cycling, horse riding to alpine skiing, ice-skating to Formula One racing. The landscape lends itself to a wealth of possibilities: the lofty Apennines become small-scale ski slopes in winter but revert to rugged open-walking countryside in spring and summer. The flat area around Ferrara is gentle cycling country, with inviting tracks etched into the raised canal banks in the Po Delta area. The Ferrara tourist authorities

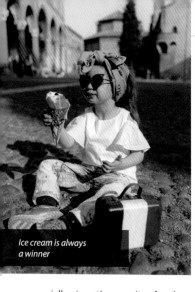
Ice cream is always a winner

have set up superb cycling routes, complete with guides, to ferry you effortlessly around the Po Delta. The region is well endowed with 'bike hotels' – places offering a full service from picnic hampers to bike repairs and maps for the next stretch of route.

CHILDREN'S BOLOGNA

Bologna is not the obvious choice for children, especially given the sparsity of parks and gardens in the centre. Active youngsters might enjoy the challenge of tackling 498 steps up the **Torre degli Asinelli**, while older ones will no doubt be fascinated by the **Teatro Anatomico** where human dissections took place, the **Specola** (Observatory) and **waxwork museums** of the University (see page 55). The innovative **Museum of History at Palazzo Pepoli** is geared to all ages with 3D films and reconstructions, and the **Sala Borsa multimedia centre**, right in the centre, is a good place to chill out with computers or films. Sports fans will no doubt be keen to watch the Virtus **basketball** squad in action, and to let off steam with a steep **climb** up the world's longest portico to the Sanctuary of the Madonna di San Luca. The best park for picnics (or snacks at the waterside *Chalet dei Giardini Margherita*, straddling the bridge over the central lake) is the **Giardini di Margherita**, just beyond the southern city walls. In the **Parco della Montagnola**, children can enjoy a variety of shows and themed activities.

WHAT'S ON

Arte Fiera Last weekend of January. Dedicated to contemporary art, with exhibitions and events throughout the city.

Children's Carnival February. Allegorical floats and parades in the city.

Children's Book Fair March. A Bolognafiere-based literary extravaganza; the most important of its kind in the world.

Live Arts Week 3rd week of April. Festival dedicated to contemporary performing arts.

Madonna di San Luca (Ascension Day). Heartfelt festival in honour of the icon of the Virgin in San Luca, with a procession through the city.

Future Film Festival May. International festival of innovative cinema.

Diverdeinverde Late May. Private gardens in Bologna and surrounding hills open to the public for three days.

Bè Bolognaestate June–September. Summer programme of music, art and theatre throughout the city.

Il Cinema Ritrovato Late June/early July. Celebration of film classics with screenings in various cinemas and on Piazza Maggiore.

Danzaurbana September. International festival dedicated to contemporary dancing.

Bologna, La Strada del Jazz Mid-September. Jazz concerts and events in the Quadrilatero.

Festa di San Petronio 4 October. Feast of the patron saint, with concerts and other events taking place from 1–4 October.

Bologna Jazz Festival October–November. Almost a month of concerts headlined by well-known Italian and international jazz artists.

Gender Bender Late October/early November. International interdisciplinary festival dedicated to gender identity and sexual orientation.

Trekking Urbano Bologna Last weekend October. Guided tours to discover Bologna and surroundings.

Cioccoshow November. Foodie event dedicated to chocolate.

Motor Show December. Showcasing cars and motorbikes galore.

New Year's Eve 31 December. DJ music, street food and the burning of an effigy ('Vecchione') herald the New Year.

FOOD AND DRINK

Italy's gastronomic capital is known as 'la Grassa' ('the fat one') for good reason. Restaurant tables groan beneath plates heaped with Parmesan-dusted hand-rolled pasta, shop ceilings are hung with ham hocks, deli windows obscured by huge wheels of cheese, food markets aromatic with fresh produce. The city has a whopping 41 products protected by the European DOP (Designazione d'Origine Protetta) – more than any other city in Italy – an abundance of excellent restaurants, a tradition of long, languid meals, and a spiralling number of cooking schools where visitors can

PARMA – HAVEN OF GASTRONOMY

Crudo di Parma (Parma ham, locally known as *prosciutto crudo*) and Parmigiano (the hard, sharp-flavoured cheese) are intricately linked because the whey – the waste product from producing Parmigiano Reggiano – forms part of the quality fodder fed to the pigs that produce Parma ham. Farmed in the Langhirino hills south of Parma, true Parma ham is branded with the five-pointed crown of the medieval dukes of Parma. The raw hind thighs are hung in drying sheds for up to 10 months, as it is thought the breeze imparts a sweet flavour to the meat – unlike cheap, mass-produced *prosciutto crudo,* which is injected with brine and artificially dried to speed up the curing process. Try it as a starter, sliced into wafer-thin slices and accompanied with bread, melon or figs. End your meal, perhaps, with slivers of superior Parmigiano Reggiano, the king of Parmesans and particularly delicious with apples, pears or a good red wine. To meet the master cheesemakers and taste their products, visit www. parmigiano-reggiano.it.

discover the art behind the local cuisine. *Tortellini* remains the city's signature pasta dish, confirmed by an international cookery competition every year to determine the finest creations by the next generation of chefs.

Tagliatelle al ragù

The beauty of the regional cuisine lies in its simplicity, the dishes robust yet refined. Unless you fall for a tourist trap, it is a challenge to eat badly in Bologna and Emilia-Romagna in general. The quality of regional ingredients is superb, and local people are so demanding that mediocrity in the kitchen is frowned upon. In the wealthy agricultural region of Emilia Romagna, each town produces its own pasta dishes and signature foods. Modena jealously guards the secrets of its world-renowned artisanal vinegar, Parma has patented Parmesan cheese and Italy's favourite ham (*prosciutto crudo di Parma*), and a trip to Ferrara can only mean lashings of *cappellacci di zucca* (pumpkin-filled pasta) or *salama da sugo* (pig's liver and tongue stuffed into a pig's bladder and cured in wine).

The region is a trailblazer in creating food and wine routes (*Strade dei Vini e dei Sapori*). While these trails are often more of a promotional tool than a genuine excuse to tickle your taste buds, the routes are a convenient way to track down the top local producers of everything from asparagus and slippery eels to Parma ham and Parmesan cheese.

Pescherie Vecchie is an epicurean enclave

WHERE TO EAT

With gastronomic treats galore in the covered Mercato di Mezzo, it is tempting to have snacks on the move. Here, you can pop into any one of the many delis to have them make you up a *padina* or *crescentina* (flat, focaccia-like bread) filled generously with finely sliced *prosciutto crudo di Parma*, *Mortadella* or *squacquerone* (fresh, tangy cream cheese). Alternatively, tapas-style bites are rustled together at food stalls, which can then be taken away or eaten at communal tables.

Main meals are served in a *ristorante*, *trattoria* or *osteria*, but the difference between the three is negligible these days. Traditionally, a *trattoria* serves up simple home-style cooking (*cucina casalinga*), while a *ristorante* is more high-end (and expensive). An *osteria*, once a tavern or old-fashioned inn serving wine and home-cooked meals, can nowadays range from classic to trendy (Modena's three-Michelin-starred *Osteria Francescana*, for instance, scooped the top spot on the World's 50 Best list of restaurants in 2018). A good pizzeria excels at proper pizza bubbling hot from a wood-fired brick oven (*a forno a legna*). The Italians prefer to eat pizza in the evening, and to wash it down with beer rather than wine. An *enoteca* or wine bar boasts a serious selection of fine wines, many available by the glass, and often served with a platter of cheese or charcuterie. Many inns or bars also serve food, especially pasta, and often have late-opening hours.

As in the rest of Italy, restaurants offer four courses: *antipasti* (hors d'oeuvres), the *primo* (first course, typically pasta in Emilia-Romagna but also risotto or soup), the *secondo* (main course of fish or meat) and the *dolce* (dessert), followed perhaps by cheese, coffee and a *digestivo*. Not that you would be expected, these days, to wade through every course.

ANTIPASTI

The most characteristic *antipasto* is a platter of assorted *salumi* – cured pork products such as tissue-thin slices of *prosciutto crudo di*

FAR FROM BALONEY

If you think of *Mortadella* as the pre-packaged, pre-sliced and over-processed cold cut (American 'bologna sausage' or 'baloney') from your local supermarket, think again. Eating *Mortadella* di Bologna in its birthplace is a completely different experience. The pork is carefully selected according to strict regulation imposed by its PGI (Protected Geographical Indication), then finely ground and flavoured with small white flecks of high-quality pork fat (from the neck of the pig), peppercorns and (sometimes) pistachios. It is then heat-cured for a few hours or several days depending on the size. Sausages are typically between 5.5kg and 6.5kg (12lbs and 14lbs), though in 1989 one weighed in at 1300kg (2864lbs) and measured a whopping 5.75m (19ft) long. A good *Mortadella* should be sliced as thinly as possible and eaten with fresh, crusty bread, best washed down with a glass of light, fruity red wine. However, it is just as enjoyable as an appetizer in small, diced cubes; as a creamy mousse with *antipasti*; or as a stuffing for Bologna's famous *tortellini*. So popular is the pink sausage that there now a food festival in Bologna entirely devoted to it: the MortadellaBò in mid-October.

Parma (Parma ham), *Mortadella*, *salami*, *coppa di testa* (brawn), *ciccioli* (pork from Parma) and, if you're lucky, *culatello di Zibello*, one of the most prized and expensive of Italy's *salumi*, produced around Zibello, south of Parma. *Salumi* might be accompanied by a slice of crumbly Parmigiano Reggiano cheese. Vegetable *antipasti* are likely to feature *peperoni* (peppers), zucchini, *melanzane* (aubergine or eggplant) and *carciofi* (artichokes).

PRIMO

Tortellini, parcels of pasta bursting with pork, ham, *Mortadella* and Parmesan cheese, is a tasty Bolognese speciality served typically in *brodo* (fragrant chicken broth) or simply slathered with butter and dusted with Parmesan. Ideally, the pasta will be handmade – you get 20 to 30 percent less filling if it's made with a machine. Other typical dishes are *tortellini* with ricotta and spinach, and *tagliatelle*, usually drowning in the true bolognese sauce – a far cry from 'spag bol'. *Ragù* is also used in the ubiquitous lasagne, another authentic dish with roots in Bologna. Look out too for regional pastas such as *passatelli*, *cappelletti* ('little hats') or the plumper version: *cappellacci*, encasing pumpkin and Parmesan, and *anolini* ('rings') stuffed with beef, parmesan and breadcrumbs, and served in broth.

Tagliatelle tresses

Tagliatelle's origins go back to the 1487 wedding feast of Lucrezia Borgia and the Duke of Ferrara. The chef behind the lavish banquet served a new type of pasta, shaped in long golden strips, to reflect the blond tresses of the bride.

SECONDI

Pork is the king of meats, served in variety of ways. Most menus will feature *cotoletta alla bolognese*, a thin slice of pork (or veal) fried in breadcrumbs and then baked with Parma ham and Parmesan cheese. *Bollito misto* is a stew of mixed meats such as flank of beef, veal or ox tongue and Italian sausages, simmered with celery, carrots and herbs, and served with different sauces. *Fritto misto alla bolognese* is a mixed fry, varying from place to place, but typically including potato croquettes, mozzarella, lamb, brains, zucchini, artichoke, cauliflower and aubergine, all dipped in batter and deep-fried. Some restaurants offer fresh fish, usually served whole or by weight, but meat

Mortadella, the prized cold cut of Bologna

dominates the menu. One of the best and most affordable places for fish is *Banco 32* in the Mercato delle Erbe, next to the fishmonger. The seating is basic, but the fish is boat-fresh, and there's a buzzy vibe.

DOLCI

Desserts range from a fruit salad or *gelato* to a choice of elaborate home-made desserts and cakes. Traditional *dolci* include *zuppa inglese* (the trifle-like 'English soup'), tiramisu, the alcohol-spiked chocolate and coffee gateau from the Veneto, and *torta di riso,* a cake made from rice, sugar, almonds and milk. Don't be surprised if you are offered *gelato* with a drizzle of balsamic vinegar – usually the superior Aceto Balsamico Tradizionale di Modena. It tastes much sweeter than ordinary balsamic vinegar and can also be used in salads, drizzled over fresh berries, or paired with honey over Parmigiano Reggiano cheese. Aceto Balsamico in its pricey artisanal form bears no resemblance to the industrial liquid often found in supermarkets.

Spag Bol?

It may seem surprising but one dish you won't find in Bologna is spaghetti bolognese. The *ragù alla bolognese,* which, in its home town, is a rich, chunky blend of minced pork and beef, veg, wine, whole milk and tomato, is used to dress *tagliatelle*, never spaghetti.

GELATI

Do as the Bolognesi do and bypass a sit-down dessert in favour of ice cream from a *gelaterie*. Locals invariably disagree on which is best but favourites include **Sorbetteria Castiglione**, Via Castiglione 44 d/e, **Gelateria Ugo**, Via San Felice 24, **Gelatauro**, Via San Vitale 98 and **Cremeria Cavour** in Piazza Cavour.

WINES

Emilia Romagna's well-deserved reputation for good living is based more on food than wine. Though huge amounts of wine are produced, the quantity outweighs the quality. Nevertheless, things have improved dramatically over the past few decades. Gone are the days of cheap, sweet, sparkling Lambrusco – at least in Italy. There are now some decent DOC dry (or off-dry), frothy Lambruscos with a pleasant acidity that goes well with the rich regional food. The Romagna side of the region, stretching east from Bologna to the coast, produces Sangiovese reds and the rather underwhelming Trebbiano whites. Sangiovese varies from thin and tart to smooth dry, ruby red and full of flavour – but, like Lambrusco, it has witnessed a dramatic improvement. The best, such as Romagna DOC, completes with Italy's finest Sangiovese. Pignoletto, from the hills around Bologna, is a delicate, affordable white that pairs well with *antipasti* and seafood. The sparkling form is a popular *aperitivo*. Restaurants invariably stock wines from other regions, such as Barolo from Piedmont or Brunello from Tuscany, and sometimes some international bottles. House wine, *vino della casa*, is usually acceptable and always reasonably priced.

TO HELP YOU ORDER

A table for one/two/three **Un tavolo per una persona/per due/per tre**

I would like... **Vorrei...**

The bill, please **Il conto, per favore**

Do you have a set menu? **Avete un menù a prezzo fisso?**

I'd like a/an/some... **Vorrei...**

beer **una birra**

bread **del pane**

butter **del burro**

coffee **un caffè**

fish **del pesce**

fruit **della frutta**

milk **del latte**

pepper **del pepe**

potatoes **delle patate**

salad **un'insalata**

salt **del sale**

soup **una minestra**

sugar **dello zucchero**

wine **del vino**

MENU READER

aglio garlic

agnello lamb

albicocche apricots

aragosta lobster

arancia orange

bistecca beefsteak

braciola chop

calamari squid

carciofi artichokes

crostacei shellfish

fegato liver

fiche figs

formaggio cheese

frutti di mare seafood

funghi mushrooms

lamponi raspberries

maiale pork

manzo beef

mela apple

melanzane aubergine

merluzzo cod

pesca peach

pollo chicken

pomodori tomatoes

prosciutto ham

rognoni kidneys

tacchino turkey

tonno tuna

uovo egg

verdure vegetables

vitello veal

vongole clams

WHERE TO EAT

Each restaurant and café reviewed in this Guide is accompanied by a price category, based on the cost of a two-course meal (or similar) for one, including a glass of wine.

€€€	over €40
€€	€30–€40
€	under €30

PIAZZA MAGGIORE AND AROUND

Ca' Pelletti € *Via Altabella 15 c/d; tel: 051-266 629; www.capellettilocandaitalia.it.* A busy little *locanda*, catering for all tastes all day: lavish breakfasts (served until noon), lovely cakes, local pasta dishes (including vegetarian), *prosciutto,* salads, and sweet and savoury *piadine* (sandwiches). Takeaway available. Informal setting and welcoming atmosphere. Mon–Fri 8am–11pm, Sat & Sun 9am–11pm.

Da Gianni €€ *Via Clavature 18; tel: 051-229 43; www.trattoria-gianni.it.* Tucked down an alley in the foodie quarter near San Petronio, this is one of Bologna's best *trattorias*, popular with both locals and in-the-know tourists. Menus are in Italian only, but staff will help you choose from the Bolognese dishes. Try the melt-in-the-mouth *tortellini in brodo*, the *tagliatelle* or *gnocchi* with *ragù bolognese* and the *bollito misto* (boiled meats – better than it sounds). Closed Mon, Sun pm & August.

Eataly €–€€€ *Via degli Orefici 19; tel: 051-095 2820; www.eataly.it.* Part of the successful Eataly emporium, this foodie store is set inside a large bookshop, with a variety of eating and drinking places on different floors. Excellent quality and choice, and a popular spot for cocktails. Mon–Sat 9am–11pm, Sun 10am–11pm.

Enoteca Storica Faccioli €–€€ *Via Altabella 15b; mobile: (0039) 349 3002939; www.enotecastoricafaccioli.it.* This historic, upmarket bar puts wine on a pedestal, while serving unpretentious, authentic local food, from cold cuts and cheeses to *crostini*, lasagne and *tortellini*. Mon–Thurs 4–10pm, Fri & Sat noon–10.30pm.

Fior di Sale €€ *Via Altabella 11d; tel: 051-281 2980; www.fiordisalebologna.it.* This inviting flower shop moonlights as a smart restaurant, serving up Italian classics with a contemporary twist. Come for the bouquets; stay for the food. Dishes are accompanied by a wide selection of excellent Italian wines. Mon–Sat 6pm–midnight.

Pappagallo €€€ *Piazza della Mercanzia 3c; tel: 051-232 807; www.alpappagallo.it.* The 'Parrot' is a charming old-world institution with fine dining, formal service and autographed photos of the many celebrities who have dined here (Sophia Loren, Gina Lollobrigida, Alfred Hitchcock, Frank Sinatra, Sharon Stone – just to name a few). The menu sticks strictly to Bolognese cuisine. If you haven't tasted the local *tortellini in brodo,* make this the place to try it. Reservations recommended. Thurs–Mon 12.30pm–3.30pm.

Rodrigo €€€ *Via della Zecca 2h; tel: 051-235 536; www.ristoranterodrigobologna.it.* In a refined palazzo formerly occupied by the National Mint, this long-established restaurant is known for its home-made pasta, fresh fish and variety of *funghi* in season (*porcini, chiodini, finferli* and more). Excellent choice of wines. Mon–Sat 12.30–3pm & 7.30pm–midnight.

Trattoria Battibecco €€€ *Via Battibecco 4; tel: 051-223 298; www.battibecco.com.* Splash out on creative dishes such as pumpkin and ginger risotto with marinated duck breast or lamb in pistachio crust with caramelized yellow onion; there are also Bolognese specialities, a good choice of fish and an excellent wine list. Hidden down a narrow alley, close to Piazza Maggiore, it has a smart wood-panelled interior and professional staff. Popular with locals; reservations recommended. Mon–Sat 8–10pm.

EAST OF PIAZZA MAGGIORE

Clorofilla € *Strada Maggiore 64c; tel: 051-235 343; www.facebook.com/ristoranteclorofilla.* Bucking the Bolognese trend, the motto here is 'Eat your way to good health', and the dishes in this unpretentious restaurant are the perfect antidote to the rich and calorific local cuisine. Expect seitan steaks, couscous, tofu, vegetable drinks, vegan dishes and diverse salads. Mon–Sat noon–3pm & 7.30–11pm.

Grassilli €€€ *Via dal Luzzo 3; tel: 051-222 961;* www.ristorantegrassilli.weebly. com. Close to the Two Towers, this elegant restaurant has the feel of an exclusive club. It was founded in 1944, and the clusters of wall-hung black-and-white photos (Luciano Pavarotti and Placido Domingo among them) recall the times when it was a popular haunt of opera singers. The cuisine is primarily Bolognese, with a few French flourishes. Limited seating, booking recommended. Mon, Tues & Thurs–Sat 12.30–2.30pm & 7.30–10.30pm.

Scaccomatto €€€ *Via Broccaindosso 63; tel: 051-263 404;* www.ristorantes-caccomatto.com. If heavy Bolognese cuisine is taking its toll, try Mario Ferrara's lighter dishes from southern Italy. The Basilicata-born chef founded the restaurant in 1987, bringing to Bologna an almost unheard-of cuisine. His artfully presented and often innovative dishes have proved very popular. Expect five- and six-course fish, meat or vegetable tasting menus. Daily 12.30–2.30pm & 7.30–10.30pm, closed both Mon & Wed lunch & all day Tues.

UNIVERSITY QUARTER

Cantina Bentivoglio € *Via Mascarella 4b; tel: 051-265 416;* www.cantinaben-tivoglio.it. Set in the lively university quarter, this trusty tavern occupies the wine cellar of the noble Palazzo Bentivoglio. For over 50 years, locals have been coming to soak up the live jazz, decent Bolognese food and laidback atmosphere. Daily 8pm–2am, lunch by reservation.

Trattoria/Pizzeria delle Belle Arti € *Via delle Belle Arti 14; tel: 051-225 581;* www.belleartitrattoriapizzeria.com. Down some steep stone steps, this exposed-brick space houses a family-run, rustic *trattoria*. Expect local dishes as well as fish and paella, Calabrian cuisine and good pizzas from the wood-fired oven. Alfresco meals on the veranda in summer. Daily lunch & dinner.

NORTH AND WEST OF PIAZZA MAGGIORE

Al Cambio €€–€€€ *Via Stalingrado 150; tel: 051-328 118;* www.ristorantceal-cambio.it. Set just outside the city walls, close to the Fiera district, this gastronomic temple serves Bolognese favourites with a creative spin. It is popular with local gourmets and foodie tourists in the know. Smart and sleek setting, warm and professional service. Mon–Fri 12.30–2.30pm & 7.30–10.30pm, Sat 7.30–10.30pm.

Altro? € *Mercato delle Erbe, Via Ugo Bassi 23–25, tel: 351-014 4191; www.al-trobologna.com.* Within the Mercato delle Erbe, this vast food hall is peppered with over a dozen outlets. Pick from an abundance of high-quality, simple eats made from market-fresh produce: delicious pizza, veggie snacks, fish dishes, soups and salads. There is waiter service for more substantial meals; otherwise it's self-service. At night, the food hall transforms into a cool spot for *aperitivos*. Tues–Thurs noon–3pm & 7–11pm, Fri noon–3pm & 7–midnight; Sat noon–3pm & 5pm–midnight, Sun noon–4pm.

Caminetto d'Oro €€ *Via de'Falegnami 4; tel: 051-263 494; www.caminet-todoro.it.* This family-run local institution rustles up fine steaks and delicious desserts. Ingredients come straight from the market, and the bread and pasta is made in-house. There's also a well-stocked wine cellar. Very popular, especially in the evenings, so be sure to reserve a table. Tues–Sat 12.30–2.30pm & 7.30–10.30pm.

Dal Biassanot €–€€ *Via Piella 16a; tel: 051-230 644; www.dalbiassanot.it.* Next door to a 'secret window' overlooking the canal, this is a warm, welcoming and very popular *trattoria* with top-notch local cuisine. Watch the *sfolgina* rolling and cutting the pasta into perfect little shapes, then tuck into mouth-watering *tortellini rosa con pinoli e prosciutto* (pink *tortellini* with pine nuts and Parma ham) or *tortellini di ricotta burro e salvia* (with butter and sage), followed perhaps by roast rabbit or wild boar. Be sure to save room for the decadent chocolate cake cloaked with mascarpone cream. Mon, Tues & Thurs–Sat noon–2.15pm & 7–10.15pm.

Da Pietro €–€€ *Via de'Falegnami 18a; tel: 051-648 6240; www.trattoriadapi-etro.it.* Warm and welcoming, this award-winning, family-run *trattoria* serves up a range of Bolognese, Emilian and Umbrian dishes, from home-made pasta to grills; truffles and mushrooms are thrown into the mix when the season permits. Nab a seat on the outdoor terrace in the summer. Mon–Sat noon–2.30pm & 7–11pm.

Del Rosso € *Via Augusto Righi 30; tel: 051-236 730; www.trattoriadelrosso. com.* Between Via dell'Indipendenza and the university quarter, this is a cheap and unpretentious *trattoria* dishing up authentic Bolognese fare. Try the *crescentine* (savoury fried bread) with Parma ham, *Mortadella* or *squacquerone* (fresh and tangy cream cheese), washed down with *vino sfuso* (wine on tap). Mon–Sat noon–3pm & 7–11pm.

Franco Rossi €€€ *Via Goito 3; tel: 051-238 818; www.ristorantefrancorossi.it.* Situated just off busy Via dell'Indipendenza, this elegant and intimate spot plates up lighter takes on classic Bolognese and Emilian cuisine – with a creative touch. There's a choice of meat or fish menus, and a fine wine list. Mon–Sat 12.30–2.30pm 7–10.30pm.

Le Stanze €–€€ *Via Borgo San Pietro 1; tel: 051-228 767*; www.lestanzecafe.it. A curious but fashionable bar-restaurant set in a deconsecrated chapel in the Bentivoglio palace. The food is fine but cannot compete with the frescoes. Tues–Sun 11am–1am.

Serghei €€ *Via Piella 12; tel: 051-233 533; www.facebook.com/trattoriaserghei.* Set in the city's secretive 'canal street', this homely Bolognese *trattoria* is strong on pasta dishes, especially *tortellini* and *tortelloni in brodo*. Popular, too, for cocktails. Mon–Fri 12.15–2.30pm & 7.30–10pm.

Trattoria Da Me €–€€ *Via San Felice 50A; tel: 051-555 486; www.trattoriadame.it.* Previously *Da Danio*, this historic *trattoria* was reopened in 2016 by Elisa, granddaughter of the celebrated original owner Danio. Like her grandfather, she produces authentic home-made Bolognese cuisine such as *tagliatelle al ragù, tortellini in brodo* and *cotoletta alla bolognese* at affordable prices. Expect a warm welcome and a charming vintage setting. Tues–Fri 12.30–2.30pm & 7.30–10pm, Sat & Sun noon–2.30pm & 7.30–10pm.

Twinside €–€€ *Via de' Falegnami 6; tel: 051-991 1797; www.twinside.net.* Run by the owners of the neighbouring *Caminetto d'Oro*, this bistro, with an attractive modern interior, has tasty, light, modern Italian dishes, along with Bolognese favourites. Beef tartare is a speciality; bread, pastry and ice cream are all home-made. Excellent range of Italian wines by the glass. Tues–Sat noon–2.30pm & 7–10.30pm.

SOUTH OF THE CENTRE

Biagi € *Via Saragozza 65; tel: 051-407 0049;* www.ristorantebiagi1937.com. Near the Saragozza Gate, this family-run restaurant, now in the third generation, has been welcoming clients since 1937. Interiors are cool and rooted in place: an eclectic mix of antique chairs; glass chandeliers; and pale wood walls hung with copper pans. Come for authentic, home-made Bolognese cuisine: *Mortadella* mousse, *tortellini in brodo* or *tagliatelle al ragù,* followed perhaps by the *cotolleta alla bolognese,* washed down with Sangiovese wine. Open Mon & Wed–Sat evenings, Sun also afternoons, closed Tues.

Drogheria della Rosa €€ *Via Cartoleria 10; tel: 051-222 529;* www.drogheri-adellarosa.it. An old pharmacy, still with its apothecary jars, has been reimagined as one of Bologna's best-known *trattorias.* The menu is short; the food simple but perfect. Pastas will include classic *tagliatelle al ragù* and perhaps *tortelli,* filled with *stracchino* and *squacquerone.* Follow on with fillet steak drizzled in aged balsamic vinegar from Modena. Mon 8–11pm, Tues–Sat noon–2pm & 8–11pm.

FERRARA

La Provvidenza €€ *Corso Ercole I d'Este 9; tel: 0532-205 187;* www.ristorante-laprovvidenza.com. This top restaurant has a gentrified rustic interior and a menu of Ferrara specialities, from *pasticcio alla ferrarese* (pasta with meat sauce) to *fritto misto di carne* (mixed grill). Tues–Sat noon–2.30pm & 8–10.30pm.

La Romantica €€ *Via Ripagrande 36; tel: 0532-765 975;* www.trattorialaro-mantica.com. A suitably romantic inn, set in the former stables of a seventeenth-century palace. Regional pasta dishes include *cappellacci di zucca,* with pumpkin, walnuts and sage; and *garganelli* with asparagus and mushrooms. Leave room for bangers-and-mash, Ferrara-style. Mon 7.45–10.30pm, Tues noon–2.30pm & 7.45–10.30pm.

MODENA

Hosteria Giusti €€–€€€ *Via Farini 75; tel: 059-222 533;* www.hosteriagiusti.it. This little gem, tucked away to the rear of a famous deli, is strong on meat, from suckling pig to cold cuts and *cotechino di Modena* (pork sausage) in *zabaglione* sauce. Rustic but elegant, and welcoming. Tues–Sat 12.30–2.15pm.

Osteria Francescana €€€ *Via Stella 2; tel: 059-223 912; www.osteriafrancescana.it.* The culinary superstar of Modena, *Francescana* is an intimate 12-table restaurant with crisp white linens, contemporary artwork and moody-hued walls. The brainchild of master chef Massimo Bottura, this three-Michelin-starred *osteria* scooped the top spot in the acclaimed World's 50 Best Restaurants in 2016 and 2018. Expect experimental, deconstructed versions of Italian classics, served in ways you couldn't imagine before you set eyes on them. Book in advance, and brace yourself for a hefty bill. Tues–Sat lunch & dinner.

PARMA

La Greppia €€–€€€ *Strada Garibaldi 39a; tel: 0521-233 686; www.facebook.com/lagreppiaparma.* This city-centre gastronomic temple creates the very best of Parma-style cuisine, from *tortelli di erbette* (vegetable pasta) to *culatello di Zibello,* the prized cured meat. Mon–Sat noon–2.30pm & 7.30–10.30pm.

Trattoria del Tribunale €–€€ *Vicolo Politi 5; tel: 0521-285 527; www.trattoriadeltribunale.it.* With ham hocks hanging from the ceiling and local wine bottles stacked on antique cabinets, this welcoming haunt is one of Parma's best-kept secrets. The central but hard-to-find inn serves the likes of *tortellini* bursting with pumpkin and herbs, or ricotta and spinach, naturally coated in Parmesan. Daily noon–3pm & 7–11pm.

RAVENNA

Ca'De Ven € *Via Corrado Ricci 24; tel: 0544-30163; www.cadeven.it.* As 'the house of wine', this quirky palazzo, with long communal tables, unsurprisingly serves good regional wines. Also does a line in rustic fare such as *piadina*, cold cuts, cheese and caramelized figs. Tues–Sun 11am–2.30pm & 6.30–10pm.

La Gardela €–€€ *Via Ponte Marino 3; tel: 0544-217 147; www.ristorantelagardela.com.*This friendly inn specializes in meat and fish grills as well as vegetable pasta dishes. Recipes shine a light on mushrooms and truffles in season. The cypress-lined summer terrace is a gem. Tues–Sun lunch & dinner.

TRAVEL ESSENTIALS

PRACTICAL INFORMATION

A

ACCESSIBLE TRAVEL

Cobblestones and stairways within palazzi are disincentives for disabled travellers to Bologna, but there is now access in most public buildings and main museums. The Bologna Welcome website (www.bolognawelcome.com/en/for-disabled-visitors) has useful information for disabled tourists, such as accessible public and private transport, free parking, accommodation, restaurants and useful links. The office also provides a handy map, *Bologna, A City for Everybody*, which marks routes for travellers with disabilities, including written itineraries with full details of the easiest access, where to find lifts, etc. A special Radio-Taxi service (tel: 051-372 727) operates 24 hours for wheelchair-users or those who need special assistance. Vehicles serving disabled persons can circulate in the ZTL (Restricted Traffic Zone), provided notice of the registration number is given to the hotel or B&B in advance to pass on to the Municipality. In the case of access not previously communicated to the authorities, details can be sent within 48 hours of entering the controlled area. Vehicles used for disabled people are not subject to parking fees.

BOforAll is an app to find accessible places in Bologna – with useful links. Alternatively, contact Accessible Italy (www.accessibleitaly.com), a non-profit organization that helps tourists with disabilities to plan their holidays in Italy.

ACCOMMODATION

Bologna has seen a burgeoning number of hotels and B&Bs in recent years, particularly those catering for tourists. However, during the major trade fairs, you'll be hard-pressed to find a place to stay unless you book well in advance. In truth, unless you are specifically travelling to Bologna for a fair, it is best to avoid a trip during these times, especially as hotel prices double or even treble. The main events are Cosmoprof (Cosmetics) in March, Fiera del Libro per Ragazzi (Children's Book Fair) in early April, Cersaie (ceramics) in late September and Saie (for the building industry) in mid-November. Outside these dates, finding a hotel room in the historic centre is generally not a problem.

The quietest periods in Bologna are the second week of January, February and mid-summer when it's very hot and many residents abandon the city for cooler climes. Some restaurants may shutter for a couple of weeks or more in August.

Bologna is littered with upmarket business hotels, many on the periphery of the city, but to gain a true sense of the city, it's best to stay in the historic core, even if it may mean paying more. Particularly appealing are the four Art Hotels (see page 137), which have cornered the market in seductive boutique hotels; all family-run, intimate, romantic hideaways set in atmospheric palaces in the pedestrianized part of town.

The centre has a good choice of B&Bs. Quality and price often compare favourably with three-star hotels, and any lack of amenities are more than compensated for by the personal welcome and the intimacy of the setting. They do, however, tend to be on the small side so early booking is essential to secure a room. If you arrive on spec, the Bologna Welcome tourist office (www.bolognawelcome.com) will advise on available accommodation and will do the booking for you.

Rates vary according to season and days of the week, as well as trade fairs. Substantial price cuts can be found in mid-winter, and also in July and August which are low season.

When making a reservation, a deposit of one night's stay, payable by credit card, is usually requested. Note that failure to inform the hotel in advance of cancellation means you will likely lose this deposit.

Finally, on top of the cost of your room, you will be required to pay Bologna's tourist tax, usually €1.50–€5 per person, per night, depending on the

I'd like a single/double room/twin beds **Vorrei una camera singola/matrimoniale/due letti singoli**
With bath/shower **con bagno/doccia**
What's the rate per night? **Quanto costa per notte?**

rates. This has to be paid directly to your hotel at the end of your stay. Children under 14 are excluded from the tax.

AIRPORT

Bologna's Guglielmo Marconi Airport (www.bologna-airport.it) is a mere 6km (4 miles) northwest of the city centre and has easy access. The Marconi Express monorail connects the airport with Bologna's central station in a mere seven minutes, running every seven minutes (daily; 5.40am–midnight). Tickets cost €9.20 one-way or €17 return, and can be bought from automatic vending machines or via www.marconiexpress.it. From early June through September, a night service catering to early or late travellers runs from 4am to 5.20am and from 12.10am to 1.30am, departing every twenty minutes.

Taxis from the airport to the Bologna Centrale train station in the city centre cost around €20–25, slightly more at night and on Sundays. The taxis at the airport have meters, but it is always wise to check first and agree on the approximate cost of your journey.

Taxis: Cotabo, tel: 051-372 727; Radio Taxi, tel: 051-4590.

B

BICYCLE HIRE

In Bologna, the uneven cobbled streets and ubiquitous pedestrian-only colonnades aren't ideal for wheels. Very few locals choose to cycle, even in the university quarter – a sharp contrast to Ferrara where cycling is a way of life. Bologna's historic centre is very compact and much of it pedestrianized, making it very easy to explore on foot. But for those who prefer two wheels, there is no shortage of bikes to hire. Walk 'n Ride by BIKEinBo (www.touremiliaromagna.it) charges €15 a day, €30 for three days (including helmet, locks, map and raincoat), and there is a delivery service with or without collection (€5 or €8, accordingly). L'Altra Babele at Via Gandusio 10 (www.laltrababele.it), close to Bologna Central Station, charges €10 a day. A valid ID and deposit are required, and there is no delivery service. Also near the station, Demetra Social Bike at Via Capo di Lucca 37, rents and repairs bikes.

Dynamo La Velostazione (https://dynamo.bo.it) organizes guided and self-guided cycle tours in Bologna in English.

The tourist office has a leaflet of cycling trails around the city (or accessible at www.comune.bologna.it). A few hotels have free bikes for the use of guests.

BUDGETING FOR YOUR TRIP

Flights to Bologna with a low-cost carrier start at around €60 return from the UK in low season, but are more commonly €130–250 return. Expect to pay €20 per person in a youth hostel, €120 upwards for a decent double room with bath, or €100 in a simple hotel or B&B. Typically, a three-course meal with wine costs from €30–40; a sandwich with a drink and coffee €8, coffee €1.50–€2.50; an *aperitivo* with nibbles or buffet included €10. Drinks at the bar are often cheaper than those served at a table. A metro or tram ticket is €1.50 if bought in advance, €2 if bought on the bus (exact cash required). Museum entrance charges range from €3–12. Entrance to state museums is free for EU citizens under 18 or over 65; and there is free-for-all entrance to state (and some other) museums on the first Sunday of the month. Look out also for complementary concerts in churches and outdoor performances in summer.

C

CAMPING

The Campeggio Città di Bologna at the Centro Turistico Città (Via Romita 12/4a, tel: 051-325 016) is close to the Fiera District but surrounded by lush greenery. A regular bus service links the campsite to Bologna Centrale train station. Bungalows and mobile homes are available, as well as a restaurant, large swimming pool in summer (free) and fitness centre (charge).

CAR HIRE

Most of Bologna's centre is closed to private traffic (see Driving), but you may want to hire a car to visit other cities of Emilia Romagna. Try Avis (Via Nicolo dall'Arca 2/D, tel: 051 634 1632); Europcar (Via Cesare Boldrini 22B, tel: 051 353

665); Maggiore (Via Cairoli 4, tel: 051 252 525); or the very competitive Sicily by Car, at the airport (tel: 051 647 2006). These major rental companies also have outlets at Bologna's G. Marconi airport, though the best rates are usually found online. Hiring a small car costs €15–50 a day, depending on the season. The cost includes third-party liability and taxes, but excludes insurance excess. Drivers must present their own national driving licence or one that is internationally recognized.

CLIMATE

Spring, early summer and early autumn are the best seasons to visit the city. The climate is hot and humid in summer, though the Apennine range can bring welcome breezes. Winters tend to be cold and wet, often with snow (particularly January and February). Lack of wind in winter also leads to fog and mist, often with high levels of air pollution. But there are also plenty of sunny days. A bonus of Bologna is the series of beautiful porticoes that allow you to walk across the city protected from rain and the sweltering heat.

	J	F	M	A	M	J	J	A	S	O	N	D
C°	6	9	13	18	21	25	27	27	24	19	13	8
F°	43	48	55	65	69	77	80	80	75	66	55	46

CLOTHING

Apart from the summer months, when all you need is light, cool clothes, bring plenty of layers, an umbrella and raincoat. In winter, don't forget a warm coat or anorak. A pair of comfortable walking shoes is essential as you'll probably spend most of your time on foot. Wear appropriate clothes when visiting churches.

CRIME

As you would in any major city, take precautions against pickpockets. Leave important documents and valuables in the hotel safe, and keep a firm hold of handbags, especially in crowded areas and on public transport. For insurance purposes, you must report theft and loss immediately to the police.

> I want to report a theft **Vorrei denunciare un furto.**
> My wallet/passport/ticket has been stolen **Mi hanno rubato il portafoglio/il passaporto/il biglietto**

D

DRIVING

Bologna is at the crossroads of major motorways and can be reached directly from many major Italian cities. The A1 from Milan turns south at Bologna towards Florence, Rome and Naples; the A13 runs north to Ferrara and Padua; the A14 connects Bologna to Rimini and other coastal resorts on the Adriatic. Unless you are visiting sites outside Bologna, a car is a drawback. The centre, which is a maze of one-way streets, is mainly a **Zona Traffico Limitato** (ZTL; restricted traffic area) from 7am to 8pm daily, with access only for residents and authorized vehicles.

In the so-called T area (via Ugo Bassi, Via Rizzoli and Via dell'Independenza), all traffic – even public transport and taxis – is forbidden at weekends, from 8am on Saturday to 10pm on Sunday. Entrance to the ZTL area is electrically monitored and vigorously enforced by the authorities. Visitors staying in the city centre are allowed access, but you must give your number plate to your hotel in advance so they can register it with the local authorities, thereby avoiding a fine.

If you're bringing your own car, you will need a valid driving licence, current insurance and, if you're a non-EU licence holder, an international driving permit. You must carry your car documents and passport while driving, and you can be fined instantaneously if you cannot present them when stopped by the police.

Road assistance: tel: 116

Parking. You can park in the **blue-zone** parking spaces (delineated by a blue line), where price and times depend on the zones (check the signs). Payment can be made with a smartphone or mobile. There are 24hr car parks on Piazza XX Settembre, adjacent to the bus station, and Piazza VIII Agosto; a full list of car parks can be found on the www.bolognawelcome.it website. If you are staying at a hotel or B&B in the city centre, you are allowed access but only by giving advance notice. Hotels in the city centre with parking facilities charge around €30 a night.

Rules of the road. Drive on the right, overtake on the left. Unless otherwise indicated, speed limits are 50kmh (30mph) in towns and built-up areas, 90kmh (55mph) on main roads and 130kmh (80mph) on motorways (*autostrade*). Headlights must be kept on during the day on motorways and state roads (*strade statali*). Seat belts are compulsory in the front and back, and children should be properly restrained. The use of hand-held mobile phones while driving is prohibited. The blood alcohol limit is 0.05 percent, and police occasionally make random breath tests.

Breakdown. In case of accident or breakdown, telephone 113 (General Emergencies) or, for the Automobile club of Italy (ACI), call 803 116 free from landline or mobile with Italian provider, or 02-6616 5593 or 06-491 115 from a mobile with a foreign provider. The ACI provides an efficient 24hour service. Note that it's obligatory to carry a warning triangle and a fluorescent jacket in case of breakdown.

Where's the nearest car park? **Dov'è il parcheggio più vicino?**
Can I park here? **Posso parcheggiare qui?**
Fill it up please **Faccia il pieno per favore**
Unleaded/diesel **senza piombo/gasolio**
I've had a breakdown **Ho avuto un guasto**
There's been an accident **C'e stato un incidente**

E

ELECTRICITY

220V/50Hz AC is standard. Sockets take two-pin, round-pronged plugs. Visitors from the UK and the US will require an adaptor or transformer.

EMBASSIES AND CONSULATES

Australian Embassy, Via Antonio Bosio, 5, 00161 Rome, tel: 06-852 721, http://italy.embassy.gov.au

Canadian Embassy, Via Zara 30, 00198 Rome, tel: 06-854 441; www.canadainternational.gc.ca

Irish Embassy, Villa Spada, Via Giacomo Medici 1, 00153 Roma, tel: 06-585 2381; www.dfa.ie/irish-embassy/italy

Honorary consulate of South Africa, Via degli Agresti, 2, 40123 Bologna, tel: 051-272 600, http://lnx.sudafrica.it

Embassy of New Zealand, Via Clitunno, 44, 00198 Rome, tel: 06-853 7501, www.mfat.govt.nz/en/countries-and-regions/europe/italy/new-zealand-embassy

British Embassy, Via XX Settembre 80/a, 00187 Rome, tel: 06-4220 0001, www.gov.uk/government/world/organisations/british-embassy-rome

US Embassy, Via Vittorio Veneto 121, 00187 Rome, tel: 06-46741, https://it.usembassy.gov

EMERGENCIES

Police 112, **Fire** 115, **Ambulance** 118, **General Emergency** 113

G

GETTING TO BOLOGNA

Bologna is well connected to the major cities of Europe. From the UK, direct flights to Bologna are operated by British Airways (www.britishairways.com) from London Heathrow; easyJet (www.easyjet.com) from London Gatwick;

and Ryanair (www.ryanair.com) from Stansted, London Luton, Edinburgh and Manchester. Flight costs vary according to the time of year and day of the week. An off-season return booked in advance with a low-cost carrier can be as little as €60 (hand-luggage only).

American Airlines (www.aa.com) operates the only direct flights (June–Sept) from North America (Philadelphia) to Bologna. Otherwise, there are many indirect flights with a change at one of the European hubs (Rome, Milan, Paris, Frankfurt or Zurich).

GUIDES AND TOURS

Two-hour walking tours of the city (€15 per person and free for children under 12) depart daily from the Bologna Welcome tourist office in Piazza Maggiore. In Italian and English, the guided tours take in the Basilica di San Petronio, the ancient market area, the Two Towers and other cultural highlights of the historic centre.

Bologna Welcome offers a host of other guided tours, both within the city and in the province of Emilia Romagna. Many of these are culinary trails of some sort: a visit to the food stores of the medieval market, a Parmigiano Reggiano cheese factory, Sangiovese wineries or a tour of Modena's prestigious balsamic vinegar production. Motor aficionados can test drive a Ferrari, visit the two Ferrari museums and see the Ducati and Lamborghini factory floors and historical collections.

Il Salotto di Penelope (www.ilsalottodipenelope.it) is one of the city's 25 cookery schools where you can learn the secrets of making Bolognese pastas and other Emilian specialities.

H

HEALTH AND MEDICAL CARE

EU citizens with a European Health Insurance Card (EHIC) are entitled to emergency medical care under the same terms as the Italian residents, as are British citizens on production of a valid Global Health Insurance Card (GHIC). UK citizens in possession of an EHIC can continue to use the card until its expiry date, at which point they should obtain a GHIC (www.dh.gov.uk). Like the EHIC, the GHIC does not cover the full cost of major treatment (or dental treatment), so it is essential to have travel insurance. You normally pay the full cost of emergency treatment upfront and claim it back upon returning home; be sure to hang onto all medical and prescription receipts to back up your claim. Nationals of other countries should check whether their government has a reciprocal health agreement, and/or ensure that they have adequate insurance cover.

The water is safe to drink but most locals drink mineral water.

If you need a doctor (*medico*), ask at a pharmacy or your hotel. For serious cases or emergencies, dial 113 for an ambulance or head for the *Pronto Soccorso* (Accident and Emergency) of the local hospital, which will also deal with emergency dental treatment.

Pharmacies. A pharmacy is identified by a green cross. Locations of after-hours pharmacies are posted on all pharmacy doors. An all-night service is available at the Farmacia Comunale at Piazza Maggiore 6 in the centre of the city.

I need a doctor/dentist **Ho bisogno di un medico/dentista**
Where is the nearest chemist? **Dov'è la farmacia più vicina?**

L

LGBTQ+ TRAVELLERS

Bologna has a long tradition of openness towards diversity and minorities. Even in the 1970s, when very few Italian towns had openly gay-friendly bars or clubs, there were meeting places in the city for the LGBTQ+ community; and in 1995, Marcello Di Folco was elected Municipal Councillor of Bologna – the first transsexual in Europe to hold public office. The Igor Libreria, Via Santa Croce 10 (at the Senape Vivaio Urbano, www.senapevivaiourbano.com), is entirely devoted to LGBTQ+ culture.

The city is the seat of Arci Gay, Italy's biggest gay-rights organization at Via Don Minzoni 18 (tel: 051-095 7241, www.arcigay.it). The venue is also home to the Cassero LGBTI+ Center – the provincial branch of Arci Gay Cassero LGBTI+ Center (www.cassero.it) – and Il Cassero, one of the city's most popular LGBTQ+ clubs.

LGBTQ+ information, including services, associations and gay-friendly bars and clubs, can be found on the tourist information website (www.bolognawelcome.com).

M

MAPS

The Bologna Welcome tourist office, at the airport or in Piazza Maggiore, supplies a useful free and updated map of the city. You are unlikely to need anything more detailed, but if you require maps for other cities or areas of Emilia Romagna, you can find them at La Feltrinelli bookshop by the Due Torri.

MEDIA

Most hotels in Bologna will provide satellite TV, broadcasting 24hr English-speaking news channels. The Italian state TV network, RAI (Radiotelevisione Italiana) broadcasts three channels, RAI 1, 2 and 3, and a huge number of private channels churning out soaps, films and quiz shows. The state-run radio stations (RAI 1, 2 and 3) mainly broadcast news, chat and music.

Details of cultural and other local events are available on the Bologna Welcome website, www.bolognawelcome.com.

National dailies such as the *Corriere della Sera* and *La Repubblica* have Bologna sections, and *Il Resto del Carlino* (www.ilrestodelcarlino.it) is almost entirely devoted to Bologna, including listings (in Italian). The main English and foreign newspapers are available on the day of publication from major newsstands.

MONEY MATTERS

Currency. In common with most other European countries, the official currency used in Italy is the euro (€), divided into 100 cents. Euro notes come in denominations of 500, 200, 100, 50, 20, 10 and 5; coins come in denominations of 2 and 1, then 50, 20, 10, 5, 2 and 1 cents.

Exchange facilities. Banks offer the best rates, followed by exchange offices (*cambi*) and hotels. Some exchange offices offer commission-free facilities, but check that the exchange rate is not exorbitant. They are usually open Mon–Sat 8.30am–7.30pm. Both the airport and railway station have exchange offices.

Credit cards and cash machines. The major international credit cards are accepted in the majority of hotels, restaurants and stores.

> I want to change some pounds/dollars **Desidero cambiare delle sterline/dei dollari**
> Can I pay with a credit card? **Posso pagare con la carta di credito?**

O

OPENING TIMES

Banks. Generally open Monday–Friday 8.30am–1.30pm and 2.30–4pm, but hours vary; some open continuously from 8am–4pm.

Museums and art galleries. Opening times vary but closing day is nearly always Monday. Some museums close over the lunch period or close early, eg at 2pm or 3pm. The tourist office on Piazza Maggiore has up-to-date lists of opening hours for museums, galleries and churches.

Churches. Usually close from noon to 3pm or later, though San Petronio is open all day.

Shops. Typically open Monday to Saturday, though many are also open on Sundays. Opening hours are traditionally 9am–1pm and 3.30–7.30pm, though many shops are now open all day. Some shops close for at least a part of August.

P

POLICE

The city police or *polizia urbana* regulate traffic and enforce laws while the *carabinieri* are the armed military police who handle law and order. In an emergency, the *carabinieri* (Via dei Bersaglieri 3) can be reached on 112 – or you can ring the general emergency number, 113. In the case of stolen goods, contact the *questura* (police station) at Piazza Galileo 7, tel: 051-640 1111.

See also Emergencies.

Where's the nearest police station? **Dov'è il posto di polizia più vicino?**

POST OFFICES

The central post office, at Piazza Minghetti 4, is open Mon–Fri 8.20am–7.05pm, Sat 8.20am–12.35pm. Most other post offices open Mon–Fri 8.20am–1.35pm, Sat 8.20am–12.35pm. Stamps can be bought at any post office or *tabaccheria*.

Where's the nearest post office? **Dov'è il l'ufficio postale più vicino?**
I would like a stamp for this letter/postcard **Desidero un francobollo per questa lettera/cartolina**

PUBLIC HOLIDAYS

1 January *Capodanno* New Year's Day
6 January *Epifani (La Befana)* Epiphany

25 April *Festa della Liberazione* Liberation Day
1 May *Festa dei lavoratori* Labour Day
2 June *Festa della Repubblica* Republic Day
15 August *Ferragosto* Assumption
4 October *San Petronio*
1 November *Ognissanti* All Saints' Day
8 December *L'Immacolata Concezione* Immaculate Conception
25 December *Natale* Christmas Day
26 December *Santo Stefano* St Stephen's Day
Moveable dates:
Pasqua Easter
Lunedì di Pasqua Easter Monday

T

TELEPHONES

When phoning abroad, dial the international code, followed by the city or area code and then the number. Note that telephone numbers within Italy are usually nine or ten digits long, but can be any amount of digits from six up to eleven. Telephone numbers beginning with 800 are free. Italian area codes are incorporated into the numbers, so even if calling within Bologna, you must include the code.

For EU citizens, roaming in Italy incurs no extra fees – you can use your phone as if you were at home. If you're from outside the EU, be sure you make the necessary arrangements with your mobile provider to avoid hefty roaming fees on your phone bill. Many UK providers include roaming, but may have a cap of around £20. If you are in Italy for some time, it's worth purchasing an Italian SIM 'pay as you go' (*scheda pre-pagata*) available from any mobile shop in Italy. To do so, you will need your passport or ID card.

TIME ZONES

Italy is one hour ahead of Greenwich Mean Time (GMT). From the last Sunday in March to the last Sunday in October, clocks are put forward by one hour.

The chart below shows times in cities across the globe when it is midday in Bologna.

New York	London	**Bologna**	Jo'burg	Sydney
6am	11am	**noon**	1pm	8pm

TIPPING

A 10 percent service charge is normally included in the restaurant bill, and a tip on top of this is not expected. Most restaurants still impose an outdated cover and bread charge (*pane e coperto*) of around €1.50–5. For quick service in bars, leave a coin or two with your till receipt when ordering. Taxi drivers do not expect a tip but always appreciate a bit extra.

Thank you, this is for you **Grazie, questo è per lei**
Keep the change **Tenga il resto**

TOILETS

The train and bus stations have public toilets, so does the Biblioteca Salaborsa on Piazza di Nettuno right in the centre. Otherwise, it is generally a case of using the facilities of a café or bar. *Signori* is men, *signore* women.

Where are the toilets, please? **Dov'è sono i gabinetti, per favore?**

TOURIST INFORMATION

Italian Tourism authority offices abroad:

Australia: Level 2, 140 William Street, East Sydney NSW 2011, tel: 02-9357 2561

Canada: 365 Bay Street, Suite 503, Toronto (Ontario) M5H 2V1, tel: 416-925 4882

UK: 1 Princes Street, London W1B 2AY, tel: 020-7408 1254

US: New York: 686 Park Avenue, 3rd Floor, New York, NY 10065, tel: 212-245 5618

Los Angeles: 10850 Wilshire Blvd, Suite 575, Los Angeles, CA 90024, tel: 310-820 1898.

The common website for all tourist offices is www.enit.it.

Bologna tourist offices

The main Bologna Welcome tourist office (Mon–Sat 9am–7pm, Sun 10am–5pm; tel: 051-658 3111) is in the heart of the city, beneath the portico of Palazzo Podestà in Piazza Maggiore. Services include hotel booking, restaurant reservations, bookings for guided tours or tickets for flights, trains, theatre, cultural and sporting events. Staff are efficient and helpful, and can supply free maps and leaflets in English. There is a second Bologna Welcome office in the Arrivals Hall of Bologna's G. Marconi airport. The tourism board also has an excellent, up-to-date website, www.bolognawelcome.com, which gives you everything you need to know for a stay in the city, from descriptions of hotels, restaurants and museums to where to go for an *aperitivo* or how to use the buses. Use the search box to make the most of it. The Bologna Welcome Card, available online or at both Bologna Welcome offices, allows you free admission to many museums, plus includes a guided walking tour of the city centre (departs daily from tourist office), access to the Asinelli tower and Palazzo Re Enzo, and discounts at numerous restaurants and shops. It is good value at €25 (Bologna Welcome Card Easy) or €40 (Bologna Welcome Card Plus); the latter also includes guided tours on the City redbus, the San Luca Express and the San Luca Sky Experience. Both cards are valid for fifteen days.

The Mibac call centre (Ministry of Cultural Heritage and Activities) is available in English, Spanish and Italian, free phone: 800 99 11 99.

TRANSPORT

The historic centre, where virtually all the attractions are located, is compact, flat and comfortably covered on foot. It is easy to find your way around with a free map from the tourist office, sheltered from the elements beneath the colonnades and orientated by the city's landmark towers.

Bus. Bologna has a good public transport network run by TPER (www.tper.it), which covers the whole city and beyond. Routes and timetables are available on the website. Tickets can be bought in advance from tobacconists, newsstands or from one of the five TPER information points in the city. A single ticket, which is valid for 75 minutes, costs €1.50 in advance, or €2 if bought from an automatic machine on board the bus (you need the exact change). Tickets bought before boarding must be validated as soon as you board the bus. A 24hr ticket with unlimited bus travel costs €5, or a city pass for ten journeys costs €12 and can be used by more than one person.

The coach station is located just 100m from Bologna Centrale train station. Coach services connect Bologna with main Italian cities, though trains tend get you there faster.

The open-top, hop-on-hop-off City redbus (www.cityredbus.com) provides a tour of the city, departing from the train station (6–11 daily, timetables on website). An audioguide provides information in eight languages. Tickets cost €15, or €22 including the San Luca Express. 'Stop and Go' tickets are valid all day. The Bologna Welcome office in Piazza Maggiore sells tickets, or buy them on board or at affiliated stores and hotels. The San Luca Express connects the city centre to the Basilica di San Luca, in season only. The City redbus tour and the San Luca Express are included in the Bologna Welcome Card Plus.

Rail. Bologna Centrale train station (Piazza Medaglie d'Oro 2, www.bolognacentrale.it) is a key hub in the Italian rail network, with high-speed trains connecting the city to Florence (30min), Milan (1hr), Venice (1.5hr) and Rome (2.5hr). Trains are also the most efficient means of transport to the cities of Emilia Romagna: Modena, Ferrara, Parma, Rimini and Ravenna. For complete online timetables and booking (in English or Italian), visit www.trenitalia.com.

The station is located about 20 minutes' walk from the historic centre, on the northern edge of the city. There are two main train companies, Trenitalia and Italo (www.italotreno.it), both offering trains out of Bologna Centrale. The ticket office is open 6am–9pm; alternatively, you can purchase tickets online or at the self-service vending machines. Tickets must be validated at the yellow machines in the station. If you have a return ticket, you must validate it twice (once going, once returning).

Taxis. Taxis cannot be hailed in the street. The main taxi ranks are located at Bologna Centrale train station and Piazza Maggiore, but there are others scattered through the city. Taxis have meters, but it is always wise to agree an approximate cost with the driver before setting off on any given journey. The fare will depend on the time of day, the day of the week and the number of pieces of luggage.

The following radio taxi companies offer a 24hr service:

Cotabo: 051-372 727
Cat: 051-4590
Cosepuri Auto Blu: 051-519 090

When's the next bus/train to...? **Quando parte il prossimo autobus/treno per...?**
single (one-way) **andata**
return **andata e ritorno**
What's the fare to..? **Qual'è la tariffa per...?**

V

VISAS AND ENTRY REQUIREMENTS

EU citizens need only a valid passport. Citizens of the UK, US, Canada, Australia and New Zealand can stay for up to three months without a visa, and can extend their stay with a visa from the Italian embassy or consulate. Under rules expected to come into effect in 2024, passport holders from over fifty non-EU countries, including the UK, the US, Canada, Australia and New Zealand, will need to apply for a European Travel Information and Authorisation System (www.etiasvisa.com) visa waiver before leaving home to visit any EU member state. The document should cost about €7, and applies to 18–70 year olds.

W

WEBSITES AND INTERNET ACCESS

www.bolognawelcome.com – official city tourist website, packed with information and advice.

www.bologna-airport.it – Bologna airport information.

www.trenitalia.com – train information.

www.tper.it – bus information.

www.emiliaromagnaturismo.it – official website for the whole region, in both Italian and English with useful links.

www.turismo.comune.parma.it – Parma tourist information.

www.ferrarainfo.com – Ferrara tourist information.

www.visitmodena.it – Modena tourist information.

www.turismo.ra.it – Ravenna tourist information.

www.riminiturismo.it – Rimini tourist information.

To find free wi-fi hotspots (indoor and outdoor), check the Iperbole Wireless Network website (www.comune.bologna.it/wireless). The map is constantly updated.

In the city centre, the tourist office on Piazza Maggiore, the archeological museum and the Biblioteca Salaborsa are all wi-fi hotspots.

Hotels generally include wi-fi in the room rates. An increasing number of cafés and restaurants provide wi-fi, with purchase of food or a drink, especially in the university quarter.

Y

YOUTH HOSTELS

The best hostel is the Ostello We_Bologna, Via de' Carracci 69/14, hello@we-bologna.it or www.hostelworld.com, tel: 051-039 7900, a highly rated design hostel 800m northwest of the station. Rooms sleeping two or four people all come with an en-suite bathroom and air conditioning. Communal areas include a kitchen, breakfast room, lounge, video room and outdoor area. There's a 24hr reception, plus free wi-fi and breakfast.

WHERE TO STAY

Bologna has a wide range of accommodation, from the large modern hotels hovering on the city's fringes aimed at business travellers to the smaller independent hotels and B&Bs peppering the historic centre. Bologna is a city for all seasons, but during the main trade fairs, hotels can be booked up months in advance and prices double or often treble. Rates tend to fall in mid-summer and are generally at their cheapest in February, the quietest month. If you arrive without a reservation, the Bologna Welcome tourist office (www.bolognawelcome.com) in Piazza Maggiore offers a free hotel-booking service.

Hotels are officially categorized from one to five stars, or, at the very top end of the scale, five-star deluxe. The ratings denote facilities (which sometimes don't exist), and are no real indicator of charm or atmosphere. The most prestigious hotel is undeniably the five-star deluxe *Grand Hotel Majestic*, a Belle Epoque headturner poised on the shores of Lake Maggiore. Some of the most appealing stays, right in the centre and blurring seamlessly into their medieval surroundings, are the *Bologna Art Hotels* – a family of three: *The Commercianti*, *Orologio* and *Novecento* (www.bolognarthotels.it). It also has a centrally located four- and five-star apartment block for self-catering breaks. B&Bs in Bologna are now plentiful but, because of space restrictions in the city centre, many of them only have one or two rooms.

Hotel rates usually include breakfast, though check first as some have started to charge it separately. Being Bologna, breakfast is usually a fairly substantial fare; think fresh fruit, Parma ham, cheeses, yoghurts and freshly baked *patisserie*. If breakfast is not included in the room rate, it is usually better value to pop out for a cappuccino and croissant in a local café.

As is the case in many of Italy's cities, a tourist tax applies to any non-resident staying in a hotel or B&B. Children under 14 are exempt. The rate is €1.50–5 per person, per night depending on the room rate, for up to a maximum of five nights. For a couple staying in a four-star hotel for three nights, expect an extra cost of around €15. The tax must be paid to the hotel before departure (it is never paid in advance either to the hotel or to a tour operator or hotel website).

Each accommodation reviewed in this Guide is accompanied by a price category, based on the cost of a standard double room in high season. Price ranges include breakfast, but exclude tourist tax.

           €€€€   **over 300 euros**
             €€€   **200–300 euros**
               €€   **120–200 euros**
                 €   **under 120 euros**

PIAZZA MAGGIORE AND AROUND

Art Hotel Commercianti €€ *Via de'Pignattari 11; tel: 051-745 7511;* www.art-hotel-commercianti.it. Set in a side street beside San Petronio, this frescoed medieval palace is home to a stylish yet seductive hotel in the very heart of the city. Well-restored communal rooms lead to romantic bedrooms beneath the eaves, many with views across the alley to the Gothic windows of San Petronio or over the rooftops. Best rooms are at the top. Excellent buffet breakfast and free bikes.

Art Hotel Corona d'Oro 1890 €€ *Via Guglielmo Oberdan 12; tel: 051-745 7611;* www.hco.it. On a cobbled pedestrianized street close to the iconic Due Torri, this peaceful bolthole is one of the most sought-after city-centre retreats. An atmospheric medieval palazzo, it is said to have housed Italy's first printing works, before being reimagined as a hotel in 1890. A Renaissance portico, sixteenth-century coffered ceilings, and the former winter garden transformed into an elegant entrance hall, all add to the charm.

Art Hotel Novecento €€ *Piazza Galileo 4/3; tel: 051-745 7311;* www.bolognarthotels.it. A chic designer hotel in Art Nouveau style right in the historic core of the city – just steps from the fountain of Neptune. Guest rooms, which include suites, overlook hidden corners of the medieval centre.

Art Hotel Orologio €€ *Via IV Novembre 10; tel: 051-745 7411;* www.bolognarthotels.it. This small, family-run, three-star hotel is much in demand for its unbeatable location beside Piazza Maggiore and for its old-world charm. Some of the guest rooms have views of the medieval Due Torri and the heart of historic Bologna.

Ca' Fosca Due Torri €€ *Via Caprarie 7; tel: 051-261 221; mobile: (00 39) 335 314761;* www.cafoscaduetorri.com. Set in the shadow of the medieval Due Torri, this is a gem of a B&B, boasting a gracious Art Nouveau-inspired interior and vistas of city towers and domes. Patrizia is a font of city knowledge and an exceptionally welcoming and helpful hostess. There's a little library, guest kitchen and a winter garden where breakfast is served. Studios also available.

Cappello Rosso €€€€ *Via de Fusari 9; tel: 051-261 891;* www.alcappellorosso. it. Exclusive hotel in the centre, set in a former tavern that was renowned for its roast partridge. There are 33 rooms, each one different, but all contemporary, sleek and equipped with luxuries such as big-screen TVs and silk kimonos. Designer rooms include: the Silent Cage Room 4'33", dedicated to the American composer John Cage; the Shock in Pink room, which pays homage to fashion icon Elsa Schiaparelli's surreal universe; and Lettera 305, a love letter to the old Lettera 22 typewriter (with a gigantic keyboard on the ceiling).

Centrale € *Via della Zecca 2; tel: 051-006 3937;* www.albergocentralebologna. it. One of Bologna's best two-star hotels: central, with clean and simple classic rooms, an excellent continental breakfast and friendly staff who go out of their way to help. Rooms are spread across the third and fourth floors (with lift) of an eighteenth-century palazzo, with fine views over the rooftops.

Delle Drapperie € *Via delle Drapperie 5; tel: 051-223 955;* www.albergodrapperie.com. Small and charming hotel in the heart of the bustling Mercato di Mezzo. A cluster of pretty rooms comes in Art Nouveau style, all in a different colour palette with lovely floral designs and a smattering of antiques. Four junior suites overlook the rooftops.

Roma €€ *Via d'Azeglio 9; tel: 051-226 322;* www.hotelroma.biz. The location of the *Roma* is hard to beat: on a smart pedestrianized street, popular for shopping and *la passeggiata*, just a few steps from the Piazza Maggiore. The hotel has a civilized atmosphere, traditional rooms and personal service. Emilian specialities are served in the *C'era Una Volta* restaurant.

Torre Prendiparte €€€€ *Piazzetta Prendiparte; mobile: (00 39) 335 5616858;* www.prendiparte.it. A unique opportunity to rent your own 60m- (197ft-) high, 900-year-old medieval tower crowned by a panoramic terrace (12 floors to climb). The living areas, with bedroom, kitchen and sitting room, are spread across three floors. Sleeping up to two people, it is popular for special occasions or a romantic and exclusive B&B for two. There's even a private chef to whip you up a candlelit dinner. This exclusive experience comes, of course, with a high price tag.

NORTH AND WEST

B&B Bologna nel Cuore €€ *Via Cesare Battisti 29; tel: 051-269 442;* www.bolognanelcuore.it. Expect a warm welcome and expert local knowledge from Maria Ketty, who has been running this B&B for ten years. There are two attractively decorated and well-equipped double rooms and two apartments with cooking facilities.

B&B Galleria del Reno € *Via Marconi 51; mobile: (00 39) 346 2214121;* www.beb.it/galleriadelreno. Simply furnished, wallet-friendly B&B with wide views of the city centre. Very convenient location between the historic centre and the station. Free wi-fi, tasty breakfasts, but shared bathroom.

Cavour € *Via Goito 4; tel: 051-228 111;* www.cavour-hotel.com. This friendly and professionally run three-star has an excellent location in a side street just off Via dell'Independenza, with plenty of good places to eat nearby. The 47 rooms vary in size and style, from standard and superior to deluxe, some with hot tubs.

Grand Hotel Majestic €€€€ *Via dell'Indipendenza 8; tel: 051-225 445;* www.grandhotelmajestic.hotelsbologna.it. An eighteenth-century seminary has been repurposed as a luxury hotel that lives up to its name. This elegant retreat provides a rendezvous for wealthy Bolognese, lured to its prestigious restaurant *I Carracci*. Many a Hollywood legend has stayed here. Inviting lounges retain their former splendour – frescoed walls, moulded ceiling, grand chandeliers – while guest rooms are a glorious collision of classical charm and contemporary luxury. The room to book: a palatial suite adorned with antiques and featuring marble bathrooms with whirlpool baths.

Il Guercino € *Via Luigi Serra; tel: 051-369 893;* www.guercino.it. This discreet, classic hotel in a quiet (although unfashionable) area is just a five-minute walk from the station; twenty to the historic centre. Rooms are comfortable and good value, though some are on the small side. Friendly, helpful staff and good breakfasts.

I Portici €€€ *Via dell'Indipendenza 69; tel: 051-42185*; www.iporticihotel.com. This restored Art Nouveau palazzo is a four-star deluxe hotel and member of the Small Luxury Hotels of the World group. The chic, minimalist interior was the work of leading Italian and international designers. Guest rooms are cool and calming, with parquet floors, pastel shades and, in the case of the deluxe rooms, Art Nouveau frescoes. Views look out over the park or Via dell'Independenza. The *Ristorante I Portici*, with original painted ceilings and an ambitious menu helmed by Michelin-starred chef Gianluca Renzi, is one of the finest in the city.

Metropolitan €€ *Via dell'Orso 6; tel: 051-229 393*; www.hotelmetropolitan. com. Popular with both business travellers and tourists, the *Metropolitan* is located smack bang between the city centre and the station. Expect fresh, contemporary Far Eastern decor, a leafy outdoor terrace, and comfortable rooms. The pick of the bunch are the cool apartments at the top; book well in advance.

Royal Carlton €€€ *Via Montebello 8; tel: 051-249 361;* www.royalhotelcarlton-bologna.com. This austere-looking tower near the station conceals an exclusive hotel with classic interiors, a plush spa and restaurant. Staff are helpful, guest rooms spacious. The professional ambience and handy location, just five minutes' walk from the station and ten from the historic centre, make it a popular choice with executives. Hotel parking on site.

Touring €€ *Via De' Mattuiani 1; tel: 051-584 305;* www.hoteltouring.it. Friendly, family-run three-star with a panoramic roof terrace looking onto the city and, beyond, the cupola of San Luca. Guest rooms vary from the older classic style to contemporary rooms and spacious suites. In the summer months, guests can wallow in the hot tub on the rooftop deck. Ten minutes' walk from Piazza Maggiore.

UNA Hotels Bologna Centro €€ *Viale Pietramellara 41/43; tel: 051-60801;* www.gruppouna.it. Right in front of the station, this modern design-led hotel comes under the Italian UNA umbrella. Chic, clean lines set off colourful panels, and minimalist furniture makes for pleasantly uncluttered rooms. Good deals out of season (but not during trade fairs).

SOUTH

Antica Casa Zucchini €€ *Via Santo Stefano 36; mobile: (00 39) 347 9110731;* www.anticacasazucchini.it. With heavy wooden doors, frescoed rooms and antique one-offs, this three-bedroom B&B is rooted in time. Near the church of Santo Stefano, *Antica Casa Zucchini* is set in a historic house, parts of which date to the mid-fifteenth century. Features include a portico with Istrian stone capitals, an eighteenth-century staircase, and painted ceilings in the rooms.

Il Convento dei Fiori di Seta €€ *Via Orfeo 34/4; tel: 051-221 697;* www.ilconventodeifioridiseta.it. A fifteenth-century nunnery turned boutique hotel on the southern edge of the city. This little bolthole has plenty of personality: vaulted rooms, original frescoes and sacred altar sculptures brought into the twenty-first century with chic lighting and mosaic tiled bathrooms. Four of the guest rooms have been fashioned out of the aisle and apse of the church; six on the upper floor are individually designed in contemporary style.

Porta San Mamolo €€ *Vicolo Del Falcone 6/8; tel: 051-583 056;* www.hotel-portasanmamolo.it. This very accommodating B&B can be found near the Porta San Mamolo on the southern fringes of the city, fifteen minutes' walk from the centre. There's a pretty courtyard garden for breakfasts in summer. Traditionally styled rooms (doubles, triples, suites) are a decent size, and some have their own terrace.

Porta Saragozza € *Viale Carlo Pepoli 26; tel: 051-644 7437;* www.portasaragozza.it. This serene B&B retreat is set in a local neighbourhod just outside the city walls. The reception rooms are studded with antiques; the two bedrooms have a shared (but spacious and modern) bathroom. Talia Franceschini is a helpful (English- and French-speaking) hostess. Cash only.

Santo Stefano € *Via Santo Stefano 84; tel: 051-308 458;* www.bedandbreakfastsantostefano.com. This B&B by the Church of Santo Stefano wins many plaudits for its location and stylish contemporary design. The quietest guest rooms overlook the courtyard, and there are also well-equipped apartments. Weekly rates available.

INDEX

THE **MINI** ROUGH GUIDE TO
BOLOGNA

First Edition 2022

Editors: Joanna Reeves and Zara Sekhavati
Updater: Joanna Reeves
Author: Susie Boulton
Picture Editors: Tom Smyth & Piotr Kala
Cartography Update: Carte
Layout: Pradeep Thapliyal
Head of DTP and Pre-Press: Katie Bennett
Head of Publishing: Kate Drynan
Photography Credits: All images Shutterstock and iStock except: Richard Mortel 5B & 57

Cover Credits: Bologna piazzas **Shutterstock**

Distribution
UK, Ireland and Europe: Apa Publications (UK) Ltd; sales@roughguides.com
United States and Canada: Ingram Publisher Services; ips@ingramcontent.com
Australia and New Zealand: Booktopia; retailer@booktopia.com.au
Worldwide: Apa Publications (UK) Ltd; sales@roughguides.com

Special Sales, Content Licensing and CoPublishing
Rough Guides can be purchased in bulk quantities at discounted prices. We can create special editions, personalised jackets and corporate imprints tailored to your needs. sales@roughguides.com; http://roughguides.com

Contact us
Every effort has been made to provide accurate information in this publication, but changes are inevitable. The publisher cannot be held responsible for any resulting loss, inconvenience or injury sustained by any traveller as a result of information or advice contained in the guide. We would appreciate it if readers would call our attention to any errors or outdated information, or if you feel we've left something out. Please send your comments with the subject line "Rough Guide Mini Bologna Update" to mail@uk.roughguides.com.